40 DAYS OF DOUBT

40
DAYS OF
DOUBT

DEVOTIONS FOR THE SKEPTIC

ERIC HUFFMAN

Abingdon Press
Nashville

40 DAYS OF DOUBT
DEVOTIONS FOR THE SKEPTIC

Copyright © 2018 by Abingdon Press

All rights reserved.

Library of Congress Cataloging-in-Publication Data

Names: Huffman, Eric, author.

Title: 40 days of doubt : devotions for the skeptic / Eric Huffman.

Other titles: Forty days of doubt

Description: Nashville : Abingdon Press, [2018]

Identifiers: LCCN 2018022201 (print) | LCCN 2018042580 (ebook) | ISBN
  9781501869143 (ebook) | ISBN 9781501869136 (pbk.)

Subjects: LCSH: Belief and doubt—Prayers and devotions. | Skepticism—Prayers
  and devotions. | Christianity—Prayers and devotions.

Classification: LCC BT774 (ebook) | LCC BT774 .H78 2018 (print) | DDC
  239—dc23

LC record available at https://urldefense.proofpoint.com/v2/url?u=https-3A__lccn.loc
.gov_2018022201&d=DwIFAg&c=_GnokDXYZpxapTjbCjzmOH7Lm2x2J46Ijwz6Yx
XCKeo&r=ox0wiE5wyqlD4NWBvXI_LEW57Ah1_xv-dTElReAYRyw&m=KOhGf8A
43koswWbAOsvZWpw1G5APVTSKlWdO-K2GHRU&s=JJwAPr46Uqrz_8NIuI6Z3Mz
PSprrrAyMANIogIucuK8&e=

18 19 20 21 22 23 24 25 26—10 9 8 7 6 5 4 3 2 1
MANUFACTURED IN THE UNITED STATES OF AMERICA

CONTENTS

Contents

To the woman who never stops talking to God—

You saw this book before I ever sat down to write it, and you saw the man who wrote it before I knew he really existed.

Every day with you is an adventure full of grace and wonder. Your determination, wit, and those big, brown eyes set my heart ablaze, now more than ever.

I love you, Geovanna Elizabeth.

WEEK 7: DOUBTS ABOUT SEX AND RELATIONSHIPS

WEEK 8: DOUBTS ABOUT RELIGION

PREFACE

I never was a very good Christian. Believe me, I tried. When I was a teenager, I remember listening to Christian radio in countless five-minute segments before switching back to sports talk or Radiohead (Millennials, ask your parents). I gave it my best effort to watch Christian movies like *Fireproof* and *The Shack* without rolling my eyes, and despite my best efforts, I failed...sometimes during the opening credits. Over the years I've probably purchased a dozen Christian devotional books, but I found them either too slick (*God just wants to make you rich!*) or too sentimental (*God just wants to hug your neck!*).

I always feared something was wrong with me for not liking what other Christian kids liked. I used to pray about it. *Why, God? Why do I find goth kids more interesting than godly ones? Why can't I like Creed as much as I like Pearl Jam? Why would I rather watch* Game of Thrones *than* 7th Heaven?

Since that time, I've learned two things about God and myself: first, if God is real then He made me the way that I am—curious and rebellious, with a knack for sarcasm. Second, I know I'm not the only one who struggles with being a "good Christian." So I wrote these devotionals for all those eye-rolling, sports talk–listening, *Game of Thrones*–loving part-time believers and full-time skeptics out there.

I know what it's like to wonder whether you're really a Christian when you feel like an outsider and your faith is holding on by a thread. I know what it's like to have more questions than answers in churches where, too often, the best questions go to die.

Sometimes I think there are two voices arguing in my head. The first voice is a cynic. He would say he's scientific or just a skeptic, but he's too biased to be a good scientist and too jaded to be a good skeptic. Scientists and skeptics may not accept your beliefs about what's true, but they're not vehemently opposed to the *existence* of Truth. The first voice wants me to believe in nothing because there's zero risk in cynicism: if you don't believe in anything, then your beliefs can never be wrong.

So whenever I see something truly majestic—a giant waterfall, for example—the first voice speaks up to remind me that, while it's a very nice waterfall, there are thousands of other waterfalls in the world, many of which are more beautiful than this, so I shouldn't get too caught up in my feelings of awe or my instinct to worship Whoever created this waterfall.

Likewise, whenever I look up at night and wonder how *any* of this is possible: existence, pleasure, love, joy, pain, and the stars—my God, the stars. There are two hundred billion of them in our small galaxy alone, and two hundred billion other galaxies, most of which are much larger than ours, each containing around two hundred billion stars, and all of which were born from a singularity no larger than the eye of a needle. *My God*, I begin to think, but the first voice interrupts again to remind me this universe is cold and indifferent, without form or purpose, an unhappy accident. *Stars are not evidence for a loving Creator; to the contrary, they're a reminder of how obviously small and insignificant our brief existence really is. Whatever feelings you're having right now are neither transcendent nor true; human emotions are merely evolutionary coping mechanisms to help us deal with our pointless lives and our inevitable deaths.*

That escalated quickly. Sorry about that.

But the good news is, there is another voice in my head, and he is a romantic. He sees the waterfall and the stars and he *knows* there's more going on here than just random luck or cosmic coping. He says things that sound ridiculous to more learned elites, like "Everything happens for a reason" and "God has a plan for your life." He believes in love and self-sacrifice, justice and forgiveness, and angels and demons. He nudges me to dive head-first into the divine mysteries of our existence, in search of Truth.

If you've ever heard these two voices shouting it out between your ears, I hope your next forty days are filled with awe and wonder, lots of questions and maybe some answers, too.

WEEK 1

DOUBTS ABOUT GOD

Do you think God ever gets stoned?
I think so . . . look at the platypus.

—*Robin Williams*

DAY 1

IS EXISTENCE REASON ENOUGH TO BELIEVE IN GOD?

A theism makes sense. I may be a Christian now, but I still think people have some very good reasons for rejecting supernatural beliefs and embracing atheism. Just think about all the innocent people in the world who are suffering right now. By the time you finish this sentence, hundreds of children will have died in places like Afghanistan and Somalia—and even in more developed nations where cancer centers treat children who are battling that vicious, indiscriminate disease.

Atheism is not irrational, especially when you consider the hackneyed arguments some Christians make to support their faith in God. Arguments like, "The universe exists, so God is obviously real," which is a lot like saying, "Coffee exists, so Juan Valdez is obviously real." Yes, coffee obviously exists, and yes, it may seem that coffee didn't just *appear* for no reason. But

1. raw coffee beans are the result of natural selection;
2. coffee farming, harvesting, and roasting processes are the results of many generations of trial and error and scientific experimentation;
3. it would be ignorant to assume that one man, Juan Valdez, is solely responsible for all the coffee just because he's the one coffee grower you know by name.

Juan Valdez is a fictional character, but even if he were real, there have been a million other coffee growers over many generations. So why can't we just say, "Coffee comes from natural processes, is fine-tuned by science, and we don't need to know *why*. More important, coffee is *amazing*, so let's just relax and enjoy our time with coffee."

Now, replace *coffee* with *the universe* and you'll see why atheism makes sense to so many people: "The universe comes from natural processes, is fine-tuned by science, and we don't need to know *why*. More important, the universe is *amazing*, so let's just relax and enjoy our time with the universe."

Sometimes I'm still tempted to think like an atheist, but deeper reflection leads to deeper truth. Coffee must come from *somewhere*, right? The grounds come from beans, the beans from plants, the plants from soil, the soil from earth, the earth from primordial gas, ice, and dust, collected and partitioned 4.5 billion years ago by gravity, and gravity from . . . OK, we have no idea where gravity comes from. We used to think it was simply a magnetic pull, until Albert Einstein showed gravity to be a curvature in the space-time continuum. Gravity actually causes space and time to bend.

Try and wrap your mind around that one for a minute, and if during that minute you happen to drift into space, near a black hole where gravity is much stronger, those sixty seconds will equal one thousand years here on Earth. And if the books and movies I've consumed are correct, you'll return to find a planet in ruins, being harvested by alien robots, while what's left of the human race subsists underground. But you'll only be sixty seconds older than you were when you left, and you'll tell them all the stories about the way things used to be. They'll make you their commander, and you'll lead the great human uprising of 3018.

But let's get back to the coffee. We all know we have more than just

3

nature and *science* to thank for this gift: coffee comes from primeval components, manipulated by gravity, fine-tuned by innumerable, impossibly perfect conditions over 4.5 billion years, nourished by nature, enhanced by science, and cultivated with care by human beings.

Now replace the word *coffee* with *my life*, and you'll begin to see why belief in God makes sense.

Today's Scripture

"What may be known about God is plain to [human beings], because God has made it plain to them. For since the creation of the world God's invisible qualities—his eternal power and divine nature—have been clearly seen, being understood from what has been made." (Romans 1:19-20a)

Today's Prayer

Creator God, when doubts fill my mind, renew my hope and joy.
(from Psalm 94:19)

DAY 2

IF GOD EXISTS, WHAT IS HE LIKE?

I f you happen to be a Christian, you were almost certainly born into a Christian family and/or a majority-Christian nation. You probably wouldn't be a Christian if you were born in Pakistan. If you were born in ancient Greece you wouldn't have believed in one God, but a pantheon of gods and goddesses. It would seem that your beliefs, whatever they are, are socially conditioned; therefore, it follows that your beliefs can't be trusted as reliable indicators of objective Truth.

If that is the case, then all beliefs are relative, and if all beliefs are relative, then no god is truly God, and no truth is universally True. But there is a major flaw in this logic. If every belief system is the artificial product of social conditioning and can't be trusted, then so is the belief that all belief systems are artificial products of social conditioning and can't be trusted. The relative truth argument is a house of cards.

The credibility of any belief system—including Christianity—should be considered based on the veracity of its arguments. People who are most reluctant to consider the Christian God often have more problems with Christians than they do with God. Such is the case of atheist author Sam Harris, who famously wrote, "Even if we accepted that our universe simply had to be designed by a designer, this would not suggest that this designer is the biblical God, or that He approves of Christianity."[1] Harris and other atheist leaders often make this logical leap: God is not real, and even if He is real, He's not the Christian God.

It's understandable why some people hate Christians and want nothing more than to discredit Christianity; many have been hurt or offended by judgmental believers. In the same book, Harris also wrote, "Christians have abused, oppressed, enslaved, insulted, tormented, tortured, and killed people in the name of God for centuries, on the basis of a theologically defensible reading of the Bible."[2] I may not agree with Harris's assessment of history but I can at least understand why some people project their negative opinions about Christians onto the question of God's existence.

But there exists in Harris's (and others') reasoning a glaring weakness, as pointed out by the very witty G. K. Chesterton in 1908:

> The modern [intellectuals] speak...about authority in religion not only as if there were no reason in it, but as if there had never been any reason for it. Apart from seeing its philosophical basis, they cannot even see its historical cause. Religious authority has often, doubtless, been oppressive or unreasonable; just as every legal system has been callous and full of a cruel apathy. It is rational to attack the police; nay, [in times of great oppression] it is glorious. But the modern critics of religious authority are like men who should attack the police without ever having heard of burglars.[3]

Chesterton's point is that a culture faces great danger whenever its intellectual elites assume the role not only of social critics, but of supreme deconstructionists. He continues, "The human intellect is free to destroy itself. Just as one generation could prevent the very existence of the next by all entering a monastery...so one set of thinkers can in some degree prevent further thinking by teaching the next generation that there is no validity in any human thought."[4]

Honest reflection about the nature of our existence is part of what makes us human. So what happens when you set your own negative experiences with religion aside and ask more basic questions, like:

> If God were real, what would we expect Him to be like?
> Would we expect the Creator to care about His
>   creatures?
> Would He crave relationships with the things He has
>   made?

When it comes to questions like these, people of all religions and people of no religion tend to find some common ground. We all agree, for example, that to love people is better than to hate them. We all agree that taking care of vulnerable people—children, the elderly, the sick, and so on—is the right thing to do. We all agree when someone makes the ultimate sacrifice, giving their life for others, they are heroes worthy of honor and praise. Most of us agree that love is the highest moral good.

It stands to reason, therefore, that if an absolute, moral Creator exists, He would reflect the highest possible good. If His essence is not love, then He would be something less than God. A true God would care about His creation, and He would be especially concerned about His weakest, most vulnerable creatures. He would be willing to lay down His life for others, without demanding anything in return. His very essence should be love.

In other words, if God is real, we should expect God to be *exactly* like Jesus, who said God personally feeds and looks after the birds, adorns flowers with beautiful "clothing," and knows what we need before we even ask (see Matthew 6:26-32). With stories like the lost sheep and the prodigal son (both in Luke 15), Jesus insisted that God desperately desires a personal relationship with His children (that's us). And by His death on the cross, Jesus revealed to the world a God who is willing to die—joyfully—for the well-being of all humanity. Even those who reject Him.

When I finally realized that Jesus represents the truest form of God the world has ever known, everything began to change for me. If you're ready for a change, too, begin by drawing a line between the silly, spiteful things some Christians have said and done and the true, loving God revealed in Jesus Christ.

Today's Scripture

"I have loved you with an everlasting love; therefore, I have continued my faithfulness to you." (the voice of God, Jeremiah 31:3)

"Whoever does not love does not know God, because God is love."

(1 John 4:8)

Today's Prayer

I confess I've judged You according to the words, attitudes, and actions of Your worshippers. Be patient with me, and help me to have the courage and the will to seek You for myself.

DAY 3

WHY DOES GOD NEED TO BE WORSHIPPED?

L et's face it: worship is weird. For many people it brings to mind all kinds of bizarre imagery, from ancient rituals like human sacrifice to people literally drinking the Kool-Aid (see Jonestown). As hard as we try to make modern worship less peculiar for people (unlimited coffee and glazed donuts, anyone?), it's still very strange human behavior.

Imagine visiting Earth from another planet on a Sunday morning. You walk into a church expecting to observe meaningful human interaction, and you see all the people sitting in rows, reciting the same words in monotone unison. These entranced humans enter, stand, sit, and exit in lockstep. Their leader clearly wields some creepy, invisible power over them because just by saying a few magic words, every head instantly drops and every eye closes until he says "amen" and they all wake up. Then he says it's time to eat some poor guy's flesh and drink His blood, so you head for the door. You snatch a donut on the way out, because not even a mortified alien can resist a platter of fresh donuts.

Why do people worship God?

Why does God need or require us to worship Him?

Wouldn't that make God, I don't know, the world's worst narcissist?

I once attended a major concert featuring a premier female singer-songwriter. I don't want to name-drop or anything, so let's just say she's *gorgeous* and it causes *bad blood* between my wife and me when I look at her. Her music fills a *blank space* in my heart beyond my *wildest dreams*

9

and I became so entranced during her show that I had to *shake it off* and remember I'm a grown man and not *twenty-two*.

It was Taylor Swift, you guys! OK, stop judging me.

When she appeared on stage, engulfed in smoke and surrounded by dancers and fireworks, it was transcendent. Everyone knew all the words, so we sang every song together. We laughed, we cried. We raised our iPhones to the sky. We lifted our hands in praise. It was maybe the best worship service I've *ever* been to.

It was right up there with that NFL playoff game I attended where, in preparation for the contest, seventy thousand men sought the favor of the football gods by offering up countless cows, swine, and birds to the heavens. In the hours that followed, we all chanted, cheered, and wept tears of joy when the evil Raiders were vanquished at last by our hometown heroes.

I left that game sure of two things: first, nothing compares to Texas barbecue, and second, everybody worships something. The brilliant author David Foster Wallace (who was an atheist for much of his life) once offered the commencement address at Kenyon College in Ohio, and he had this to say about worship:

> In the day-to-day trenches of adult life, there is actually no such thing as atheism. There is no such thing as not worshipping. Everybody worships. The only choice we get is what to worship. And the best reason for choosing a God to worship is that pretty much anything else you worship will eat you alive. If you worship money and things—if they are where you tap real meaning in life—then you will never have enough. Worship your own body and beauty and sexual allure and you will always feel ugly, and when time and age start showing, you will die a million deaths before they finally plant you. Worship power— you will feel weak and afraid, and you will need ever more power over others to keep the fear at bay. Worship your intellect, being seen as

smart—you will end up feeling stupid, a fraud, always on the verge of being found out. And so on. The insidious thing about these forms of worship is that they are unconscious. They are default settings.[5]

A few years after delivering this address, Wallace took his own life, but he left us with the staggering notion that absolutely everyone worships absolutely, and if you worship anything but the Absolute, it will eat you alive.

We choose to worship God—specifically the God of the Bible, who revealed Himself to us as Jesus—because we want love to be our default setting.

Today's Scripture

"Oh come, let us worship and bow down; let us kneel before the LORD, our Maker." (Psalm 95:6 NKJV)

"Above all else put on love, which binds everything together in perfect harmony. And let the peace of Christ rule in your hearts, to which indeed you were called in one body. And be thankful. Let the word of Christ dwell in you richly...and whatever you do, in word or deed, do everything in the name of the Lord Jesus, giving thanks to God the Father through him." (Colossians 3:14-17 ESV)

Today's Prayer

I've tried worshipping just about everything *except* You, God, and I still feel incomplete. Today I choose to worship You by putting You at the center of my life.

DAY 4

WHY HAVE PEOPLE ALWAYS DESIRED GOD?

It's true that most everybody in human history—across all times and places—has believed in a god or many gods, but is that really evidence for God's existence? People used to believe the Earth was the center of the universe and the best way to cure a cold was to let a pouchful of leeches suck all your "bad blood" out. Just because everyone believes something doesn't make it true.

To many skeptics, it seems obvious that humanity's historic need for God was evolutionary: we believed in gods because, at some point in our past, such faith was beneficial to our survival as a species. Religion was nothing more than a function of Darwinian natural selection. But the skeptic will say those days are gone; human survival is no longer aided by belief in God or gods. In 2010, Larry King asked renowned scientist Stephen Hawking about God, and his response summarized modern academia's most prevalent sentiments about religion. "Science can explain the universe without the need for a creator," Hawking said. "The scientific account is complete. Theology is unnecessary."[6]

So it would seem that whatever religious beliefs remain are the useless leftovers of our primeval past. Like wings on an ostrich or nipples on a man, faith in gods once served a purpose, but now it's nothing more than an evolutionary misfire.

That argument used to make sense to me, and if you already hate religion, it can be cathartic to believe theology is nothing more than a

12

relic from a bygone era. But are we really prepared to so boldly conde-scend the beliefs and longings of billions of people over thousands of years into something as crude and meaningless as ostrich wings and male nipples? Are we willing to say that all supernatural beliefs are noth-ing more than misguided, biological holdovers from our cave-dwelling days?

Such an argument fails to get to the heart of the matter: *desire*. What is the origin of human desire? More important, what is the origin of our near-universal desire for God?

Think about other universal or widespread human desires like hun-ger, thirst, sex, companionship, and beauty. Each of these desires has a real and satisfying endpoint: food, water, procreation, pleasure, friends, and art, for example. We aren't capable of *craving* something that doesn't really *exist*—we wouldn't know where to begin!

Christian author N. T. Wright once explained this truism by telling a story about the night he had a powerful dream, but when he awoke, he couldn't remember what the dream was about. "Our passion for justice often seems like that," he wrote.

> We dream the dream of justice...a world put to rights...where we not only know what we ought to do but actually do it. And then we wake up and come back to reality. But what are we hearing when we're dreaming that dream? It's as though we can hear...a voice speaking about justice, about things being put to rights...the voice goes on, calling us, beckoning us, luring us to think that there might be such a thing as justice.[7]

Maybe we believe in esoteric ideals like justice, hope, and love because we know, somewhere in this world, justice, hope, and love exist.

The same logic applies to theology. Why have humans always longed for God? Maybe it's because that desire, like every other human longing, has a satisfying endpoint. We desire God because God is real.

Today's Scripture

"Yet for us there is but one God, the Father, from whom all things came and for whom we live; and there is but one LORD, Jesus Christ, through whom are all things came and through whom we live."

(1 Corinthians 8:6)

Today's Prayer

You have made me for Yourself, O Lord, and my heart is restless until it rests in you. (Adapted from St. Augustine's *Confessions*, Book 1, Part 1, AD 350)

DAY 5

Why Would God Care What I Have to Say?

I recently interviewed an atheist who used to be a pastor. In fact, he's the son of one of the most famous Christian evangelists in the world. When I asked him what led to his decision to leave Christianity, he said, "I just kept praying for people, and nothing would happen. For me, it wasn't about hypocritical Christians or anything; it was just, like, 10,000 unanswered prayers."[8]

I know a lot of people who believe in the power of prayer. Many well-intentioned Christians think they can change God's mind and bend His will when they pray. These people pray as if their lives depend on it. They also listen, because they believe God often talks back to them. Many skeptics equate such behavior with insanity. Upon learning that Vice President Mike Pence believes Jesus sometimes tells him what to do, a popular comedian and TV show host quipped, "It's one thing to talk to Jesus. It's another thing when Jesus talks to you. That's called mental illness, if I'm not correct, hearing voices."[9]

Even though I'm a pastor now, prayer still feels like insanity some days. I want to be a "prayer warrior" like so many of the Christians I admire, but sometimes I can't help feeling like people who pray to change God's mind are delusional, narcissistic, or both. Even if God exists, why would any individual's prayers cause God to change His mind? Do we even want to believe in a God who adjusts His entire business model based on a few negative customer service reviews? Why should God care what we have to say?

I've heard there are two kinds of people in the world: those who lead with their heads, and those who lead with their hearts. Head-people tend to rationalize everything. Before *feeling* something in their hearts, they have to process it in their minds. Heart-people go with their gut: before they *know* something is true, they first need to *feel* that it's right.

Many skeptics are head-people. I'd much rather *think* than *feel*, even while praying. I'm pretty good at thought-prayer: reflecting on God while gazing at the stars, or critically analyzing the Bible in search of meaning. I'm not as comfortable with heart-stuff: opening up, showing emotion, carrying on an intimate conversation.

While there are plenty of examples of head-prayer in the Bible (see Isaiah 40:8; Psalm 90:2; 111:2), the Scriptures don't entirely let head-cases like me off the hook. The primary focus and foundation of prayer in the Bible is the heart, not the head.

When Jesus taught His disciples how to pray, He began with "Our Father…" The word He used for father is *Abba*, the most casual, intimate Aramaic word for "father," which could be more accurately translated as "daddy." I presume the Bible translators couldn't bring themselves to start the most important prayer in the Good Book with "Dear Daddy…"

Nevertheless, that's how Jesus started His Model Prayer. Not with "Almighty God," "King," "Lord God," or "Master." Not even with "Our Father," really. Just *Daddy*, a word so tender and personal that most adults can't even say it out loud without giggling.

Go ahead; try it. Get down on your knees and start a prayer by saying, "Hi, Daddy." Weird, right?

It's weird because most of us think we're too grown up for God to be like a daddy to us. But Jesus was a grown man in His thirties, and He called God "Daddy" and asked for basic things like food, forgiveness, and protection. So one of two things must be true: either I'm more sophisticated and knowledgeable about prayer than Jesus, and I know more about God than He does, or Jesus knew that God wants the kind of relationship a good Father has with His kids.

When you love your Father enough to talk to Him, or just to spend time with Him and to know Him, He'll always be your Daddy, no matter how grown up you get. And He'll *always* want to hear what you have to say.

Today's Scripture

"And I tell you, ask, and it will be given to you; seek, and you will find; knock, and it will be opened to you." (Luke 11:9 ESV)

Today's Prayer

Abba, it's hard for me to be so tender. It's hard for me to pray with my heart. So I'll just say this: I want what You want. I want to trust You like a child knows his or her dad. Thanks for being patient with me.

WEEK 2

DOUBTS ABOUT JESUS

When people say, you know, "Good teacher," "Prophet," "Really nice guy" . . . this is not how Jesus thought of Himself. So you're left with a challenge in that, which is either Jesus was who he said he was or a complete and utter nut case. You have to make a choice on that.

—Bono

DAY 6

WHY CHOOSE CHRISTIANITY OVER ALL OTHER RELIGIONS?

Some people are superstitious, I guess, but not me. If I cross paths with a black cat this morning, I'm not going to think, "Oh no, it's a black cat!" I'll probably just think, "Oh gross, it's a cat."

I'm anti-cat and anti-superstition. When you think about it, religions can seem like slightly different variations of the same old superstitious tales (creation narrative, flood myth, an angry god, frightened people, a miraculous hero, an eternal reward for some, and damned punishment for others). Sometimes I wonder why anyone with any knowledge of human civilizations would ever subject himself to a single, closed religious system. What makes one religion right, and all the others wrong?

If you've ever wondered the same, I think you're in good company because Jesus also spent a lot of time deconstructing organized religion. He criticized preachers for praying long, elaborate prayers (see Matthew 6:5), condemned religious elites for using the Bible to manipulate ordinary folks (see Mark 3:1-6), hated the hypocrisy of corrupt priests (see Matthew 23:13-14), despised the assumptions made by religious leaders about who will be in heaven and who is deserving of hell (see Luke 14:15-24), and even got crazy-violent when he saw how the gatekeepers of organized religion made the sanctuary a marketplace where winners and losers were determined by the financial value of their offerings (see Matthew 21:12-17).

Jesus was determined to put religion in its place by setting the record straight about the Bible. The Bible is not just another religious book; it holds some major distinctions that deserve genuine consideration. Obviously there is plenty of religion in the Bible, but within the text, there is also a clear and distinct movement toward something called *gospel*. And gospel is not religion.

Whereas religion is essentially a collective bargaining agreement with God (if we're good to Him, He'll be good to us), gospel is essentially a free gift. (God is already satisfied with us, so in response to His great love, we want to satisfy Him all the more.) Many people tend to think of gospel as merely the Christian version of religion, but that is not the case.

Whatever ill will you might feel toward organized religion, Jesus felt it even more. If religious people have judged or punished you in some way, I promise you they judged and punished Jesus even more. I believe He endured the scrutiny and shame of religious judgment to tear the veil off of religion and show the world, once and for all, the true face of God.

The gods of religion say, "My love is based on your devotion," but the one true God says, "Regardless of your devotion, or your lack of devotion, I love you the same." How radical is the love of God? He loves Osama bin Laden and Mother Teresa the same. He loves Hillary Clinton and Donald Trump the same. He loves the Beatles and Nickelback the same. He even loves cats as much as dogs; if that doesn't prove the extravagance of God's love, I don't know what will.

How can such great love exist? Why isn't love reserved only for the lovable? Because God is not merely religious; He is pro-gospel. Jesus would never coerce you to submit to His religion so you can be accepted into heaven instead of hell one day; He simply invites you to follow Him because, in His eyes, you're already accepted today.

Today's Scripture

"And [Jesus] said to them, 'Go into all the world and preach the gospel to all creation.'" (Mark 16:15)

Today's Prayer

I've never believed in religion, but part of me has always believed in Jesus. Give me the courage to follow You today, not just with my thoughts, but with my life. When my family, friends, and others see me today, let them see the gospel.

DAY 7

WHY DO CHRISTIANS BELIEVE JESUS IS THE ONLY WAY TO GOD?

I just watched on CNN as a United States senator and former major-party presidential candidate publicly rebuked a man during a hearing that was intended to determine his fitness to serve in the Office of Management and Budget. A few years ago, the man said that, as a professing Christian, he abides by the classical church doctrine that salvation comes through Christ alone.

"You said you believe Muslims will stand condemned," the senator snapped. "Do you not see how your statement is Islamophobic?"

The foundation of such a question is the feeling that when Christians—or any other religious group—decide their way is *the* way, bad things happen in society. Crusades, inquisitions, terrorism, war, and Tim Tebow in the NFL. Isn't it cruel and moronic to suggest that those who die without first accepting Jesus as their Lord and Savior will forever burn in fiery anguish? Isn't it arrogant and wrong for Christians to say, "My religion is superior to yours"?

Haven't these religions made the world a more dangerous place? Historically speaking, hasn't the church caused more death and destruction than anything else on earth?

There's no denying that religions have, through the course of human history, been a source of violence and oppression. And while one could counter such a claim with plenty of evidence pointing to the many virtues of religion, that's just not the point.

The point is that many people don't like religion, but just because you don't *like* something doesn't make it untrue. The narrative goes this way: "Anyone who believes their religion is superior must be a bigot and/ or a fool; therefore, their religion must be false."

Or more specifically: "Someone who believes in Jesus as the only way to God is clearly not a good (or kind, or educated, or compassionate) person, and because such bad people believe Jesus is the only way to God, Christian beliefs must also be bad."

This line of thinking reflects a logical problem called the argument ad hominem, which is defined as "a general category of fallacies in which a claim or argument is rejected on the basis of some irrelevant fact about the author of or the person presenting the claim or argument."[1]

I know some Christians are arrogant jerks, but the Truth of Christianity doesn't rest on some fundamentalist's inability to take a joke on Facebook. Truth is just Truth. Any skeptic who suggests that Christians are arrogant because we believe we're right and everyone else is wrong must then explain how he reached the conclusion that he is right (about pluralism and relativism), everyone else is wrong (most of all Christians), and how that doesn't make him an arrogant jerk, too (whose beliefs must therefore, by the skeptic's own logic, be false).

That said, I really do understand why the question, *Is Jesus the only way to heaven?* induces such anxiety. I think we need to ask a better question: *Who is Jesus?*

Jesus said He was not just a man, but God in the flesh. He called Himself "Lord of the Sabbath" (Mark 2:28 NKJV), said He was hanging out with Abraham in heaven before coming to earth (see John 8:56), and nearly got stoned to death for claiming to be God (see John 10:33). These claims (and many others Jesus made) far surpass those made by Muhammad, Gautama Buddha, Joseph Smith, Moses, or any other major religious leader. Jesus wasn't just pointing people *toward* God; He was saying, "I *am* God."

You can't sincerely follow Jesus as if He's just another popular religious prophet. He either is God, or He's not. And if He's not, then He can't then just become a nice guy with a great message, because His message is entirely predicated on Him being, you know, *God*. So we don't have the option of taking the stuff we like—the Golden Rule and the good Samaritan, for example—and leaving all the stuff that makes us uncomfortable, the "Hey guys, I'm God" stuff.

It all comes as a package deal; take it or leave it.

That's why, for Christians, asking, *Is Jesus the only way to God?* is a simple syntax error. It's like asking "Is New York the only way to the Big Apple?" It's logically evident that if Jesus is God then the path to God is Jesus, and vice versa.

That's why I get so frustrated when Christians use "Jesus is the only way to heaven" as a religious weapon or an unholy ultimatum. I once saw a billboard on a rural highway that read, "Jesus is all you need! Turn or burn!" I wonder how many people saw that sign and thought, *That's an uplifting message! Maybe I should become a Christian.*

I'm sorry some believers have turned something so beautiful (Jesus is the eternal, loving God, and He came to share a message of hope with the world. Then He died on the cross and rose from the grave so no one ever has to be afraid of sin, shame, or even death!) into something so hateful (Join our church or burn in hell!).

Saying "Jesus is the only way to God" is much different than saying "Our version of the Christian religion is the only way to God." You can know Jesus without ever stepping foot in a church building. Just open your Bible (or Bible app) to one of the four Gospels and start reading. Study Jesus's words and actions for yourself. Write down your questions and share your doubts with someone you trust. It's never really been about religion; with God, it's all about relationship.

Today's Scripture

"For God so loved the world that he gave his one and only Son, that whoever believes in him shall not perish but have eternal life." (John 3:16)

Today's Prayer

Jesus, I'm not sure where I stand with religion, but I trust you enough to want you at the center of my life. Help me swallow my pride. I want to make your grace and goodness known today, by my words, thoughts, and actions.

DAY 8

WHY IS JESUS'S STORY SO SIMILAR TO OTHER ANCIENT MYTHS?

If you've studied ancient mythologies (or if you've seen conspiracy-driven documentaries like *Zeitgeist*), the stories of Jesus's life may sound familiar...a little too familiar. Narratives about His miraculous conception and virgin birth, His baptism and miracles, and His death and resurrection seem to be borrowed from older myths. That's because Jesus wasn't the first and only god-man who was supposedly born of a virgin on December 25, under a prominent star, and later visited by "three kings."

Or so we've been told.

Some of Christianity's critics accuse Jesus's followers of fabricating His story by borrowing from older narratives, such as the one about Attis, the Greco-Roman god of vegetation. Attis is said to have been born of a virgin on December 25, 400 BC. As an infant, Attis was visited by three kings. By age twelve, he was a great teacher, and later in life, he had twelve disciples.

The Hindu god Krishna (800 BC) was also "virgin-born," baptized at thirty, was called the "lamb of God," and was crucified between two thieves. The ancient Egyptian god Osiris was resurrected from the dead. The Greek god of the grape harvest, Dionysus, was born on December 25 and was crucified and rose from the grave.

Some scholars wonder if Jesus ever really existed, or if he was merely the Hebrew version of ancient pagan mythology. Given all the evidence that the Gospels are merely copies of older myths, why would any educated person pin all their hopes on Jesus?

This common critique of Christianity has been called "The Pagan Copycat Theory," and these are regular talking points in comparative religion and philosophy courses on college campuses all across America. Here's the only problem: every single argument made by copycat theorists lacks merit and proof.

Attis—a mythical, fictional, god-character—wasn't virgin-born; he was "conceived" when the god Agdistis was castrated and his male organ became the seed of an almond tree. Attis's mother, Nana, picked almonds from the tree and was impregnated by the almonds. Nowhere in history is she described as a virgin.

Attis also wasn't visited by three kings, didn't become a teacher by age twelve, and didn't have twelve disciples. Krishna's mom had eight kids before having him (so yeah . . . about that "virgin" label), he was never baptized or called "the lamb of God" during his lifetime, and he was never crucified. He "died" in a hunting accident. The Christlike legends weren't added to Krishna's résumé until centuries after the life of Jesus.

Osiris, another mythical figure, didn't "come back to life." Dionysus wasn't crucified; he was dismembered and devoured by the Titans—fictionally speaking, of course. Again, the events reminiscent of Jesus were added to the Dionysus myth long after Jesus walked the earth.

All the copycat claims about Jesus's December 25 birthday or the "three kings" are irrelevant because the Bible doesn't say when Jesus was born or anything about "three kings." A group (we don't know how many) of astrologers (not kings) brought Jesus three gifts—gold, frankincense, and myrrh. At the time, Jesus was two years old, which meant he probably just played with the boxes the gifts came in before throwing a tantrum and taking a nap.

Finally, no honest historian doubts Jesus really lived; there is just too much evidence to support His historical existence. Agnostic scholar Dr. Bart Ehrman investigated all claims made against Jesus's existence and surmised, "The idea that Jesus did not exist is a modern notion. It has no ancient precedents. It was made up in the eighteenth century. One might as well call it a modern myth, the myth of the mythical Jesus."[2]

How are these lies allowed to live on? As I discovered when I finally converted to Christianity at thirty-four, there is a shameless, bold, concerted effort in some secular circles to discredit Jesus by repeating claims like these until they've been said so often, and by so many intelligent people, that they become irrefutable.

In spite of their best efforts, however, the gospel of Jesus continues to spread like wildfire. Why? Because unlike their narratives, His story is true. At one distinct point in history, the timeless, boundless God broke into time and space and, confined by human skin, Jesus walked among us and loved us to death.

But not even death could kill Him. And if death couldn't keep Him down, a few petty lies circulated by spiteful elitists don't stand a chance. Simply trust Jesus, and build your life around His.

Today's Scripture

"He is the image of the invisible God, the firstborn of all creation. For by Him all things were created that are in heaven and that are on earth, visible and invisible, whether thrones or dominions or principalities or powers. All things were created through Him and for Him. And he is before all things, and in Him all things consist." (Colossians 1:15-16 NKJV)

Today's Prayer

I pray for wisdom to discern truth from lies today, and when the truth isn't immediately clear, grant me the determination to search for it.

DAY 9

WHY DID JESUS HAVE TO DIE?

E ver wonder why Christians are so obsessed with blood? When I used to get bored at church, I would flip through the hymnal and look for the craziest song titles I could find.

> "Nothing but the Blood of Jesus!"
> "Oh, the Blood of Jesus!"
> "There Is Power in the Blood!"
> "There Is a Fountain Filled with Blood"
> "The Blood of the Lamb"
> "Are You Washed in the Blood of the Lamb?"

What kind of a weird cult sings songs about taking baths in fountains of lamb's blood? The Christian gore fixation is clearly connected to the awful, bloody death of Jesus, but why did Jesus have to die such a violent death? Christians say "so our sins will be forgiven," but that doesn't really answer the question. God certainly didn't need Jesus to die in order to forgive us. Was He just so mad that He had to take it out on somebody, so instead of hurting us, He abused His own kid?

Does anyone else see the problem with this?

To the typical skeptic, all this bloodthirst makes God sound punitive and small, like the pagan gods of old. How can any modern, thinking person believe in a medieval religion like this, where innocent blood is needed to atone for sin and satisfy God's wrath? *Why did Jesus have to die?*

While it's certainly very weird—the blood, the wrath, God's Son on a cross—we really need to understand the context. The story of Jesus on the cross began some twelve hundred years before His death, when the Hebrew people suffered as slaves in Egypt. Ten times God told Pharaoh to let the slaves, His people, go but Pharaoh refused.

God sent ten curses to Egypt, the tenth of which meant death would come upon every Egyptian home. God told the Hebrew people to mark their doors with lamb's blood because Death would *pass over* their houses. That night, Pharaoh freed the slaves and every year since, the Jewish people have celebrated the Passover to remember the time God broke their chains by the precious blood of a lamb.

Jesus sat down to eat the Passover meal in Jerusalem with His friends twelve hundred years after the Exodus. Those men had eaten the same meal and recited the same words in the very same way every year of their lives to recall their forefathers' great escape.

But this time was different. Instead of following the script and saying, "This is the bread of our affliction," Jesus broke the bread and said, "This is my body." Then he took the wine and said, "This is my blood of the covenant, which is poured out for many *for the forgiveness of sins*" (Matthew 26:26-28, emphasis added).

And there it is: Jesus took His people's most sacred night and flipped the script by calling out sin as the new Pharaoh enslaving us. Then He referred to Himself as the lamb whose blood has the power to set us free.

Why did Jesus have to die? *To send a message about forgiveness.*

Why did forgiveness require such a sacrifice? *Because real forgiveness is always a sacrifice.*

When someone hurts you, you *know* he or she owes you. Our entire legal system is based on that premise. If that person steals from you or wrecks your car, he or she is in your debt. You can retaliate by suing, punishing, or doing nothing until resentment eats you alive. Or you can forgive what that person owes you, which means paying his or her debt out of your own pocket.

Christians believe sin works the same way. By God's grace, you have breath in your lungs and food on your table. You have family and friends who love you. You have a life and a connection to God and creation that you did nothing to deserve. The only appropriate response would be to live with a sense of childlike joy and gratitude before God.

But we've all taken God and His gifts for granted, which creates an imbalance in the universe—a cosmic debt, if you will. Every ungrateful thought, every selfish choice, and every day we live with a sense of entitlement leads us deeper into debt. Damages are owed, and we are liable.

God could have put us on trial, punished us, or He could have pulled back and quietly hated us from a distance. But He chose to forgive. It's impossible to quantify the collective debt we should owe; the damages caused by every human sin in the past, present, and future are unfathomable.

How could God forgive such an insurmountable debt? By offering the most precious gift on earth: blood spilled from the most sacred body: His. Just before He died on the cross, Jesus said, "It is finished" (John 19:30). The people there thought He was talking about His life, but really He was talking about their debt. And yours. It is finished; you're free.

That night, at the end of the Passover meal, Jesus asked His disciples to remember Him, and from then on, every time His disciples have broken bread and shared wine together, we have recalled the time God broke our chains by the precious blood of the Lamb.

Today's Scripture

"When you were dead in your sins…, God made you alive with Christ. He forgave us all our sins, having canceled the charge of our legal indebtedness, which stood against us and condemned us; he has taken it away, nailing it to the cross." (Colossians 2:13-14)

Today's Prayer

Thank You. (Repeat as necessary.)

DAY 10

DO CHRISTIANS REALLY BELIEVE JESUS ROSE FROM THE DEAD?

L iberal Christian author Marcus Borg wrote, "The central meaning of Easter is not about whether something happened to the corpse of Jesus. Its central meanings are that Jesus continues to be known."[3] Is Borg right? Does it really not matter if Jesus's physical body never left the tomb? Clearly, the Resurrection is a story based on historical events, but was the "empty tomb" merely a meaningful embellishment that told a timeless truth about love outlasting hate and life overcoming death?

Can you really be a Christian if you accept the Resurrection metaphorically but not literally?

During my first ten years as a pastor, I believed the Resurrection was an allegory. What mattered wasn't that Jesus actually rose; it was that His followers—the church—rose up in the wake of His death. It wasn't important to me whether Jesus's tomb was literally empty; His philosophy and His community were enough for me.

But after an existential crisis, I set aside most of what I'd learned in college and seminary and went on a quest for truth. I read every book written by famous atheists Richard Dawkins, Sam Harris, and Christopher Hitchens, and compared them with everything I could find from Christian authors Augustine, C. S. Lewis, and N. T. Wright. After that, I traveled to the Holy Land, and on that trip I discovered some damning evidence against my "allegorical resurrection" theory:

1. The early witnesses. Just about everyone who knew Jesus personally became convinced He was God in the flesh and that He rose from the grave. For the first Christians, the question of a metaphorical "resurrection" was a nonstarter. Paul wrote, "If it is preached that Christ has been raised from the dead, how can some of you say that there is no resurrection of the dead? If there is no resurrection of the dead, then not even Christ has been raised. And if Christ has not been raised, our preaching is useless and so is your faith" (1 Corinthians 15:12-15).

2. The graffiti. Inside the disciple Peter's house in Capernaum, archaeologists unearthed evidence of Christian worship during the years immediately following Jesus's death (AD 40s–50s). The writing was literally on the wall: etchings that read "God Jesus Christ" and "Christ have mercy." Similar writings were discovered in Nazareth, identifying Mary as the "mother of God." The first Christians didn't just *remember* or *follow* Jesus the man; *they worshipped Him as God.*

3. James. Jesus's little brother, James, was not one of His disciples; in fact, before Jesus died, James tried to stop Jesus from teaching because he thought his big brother was insane (see Mark 3:21). But just after the Resurrection, James became the leader of the church in Jerusalem for thirty years until he was arrested and publicly executed for believing in Jesus. If you've got a brother, let me ask you a question: what would it take to convince you that your brother is your God? What would it take for you to become so completely convinced in His divinity that you would die a painful, humiliating death for your belief in Him? Would an allegorical "He lives on in all of us" resurrection metaphor be enough to convince you? No. Nothing short of seeing Him rise from the dead would be sufficient.

4. The explosion. How did eleven ordinary guys become ten thousand committed disciples in the year following Jesus's death? How did the movement gain so much momentum, especially as ten of the eleven charter members (the disciples) were crucified, burned, or stoned to death by AD 70? How did ten thousand become one million by the end of the first century? And how did one million become 3.3 billion today? I really struggle to believe that a metaphysical allegory can do that. Real-life, flesh-and-bone, God-among-us resurrection did that.

I remember standing on the shore at the Sea of Galilee after weighing all the evidence, and whispering to myself, "It's real. My God, it all really happened." It wasn't an easy thing for me to admit; I had built my reputation on the idea that I knew more about Jesus than the New Testament authors did. But once I said it out loud, I knew my life could never be the same.

Today's Scripture

"See to it that no one takes you captive through philosophy and empty deceit, according to human tradition, according to the elemental spirits of the world, and not according to Christ. For in him the whole fullness of deity dwells bodily, and you have come to fullness in him ... when you were buried with him in baptism, you were also raised with him through faith in the power of God, who raised him from the dead."

(Colossians 2:8-12 ESV)

Today's Prayer

I've tried rationalizing You. I've tried boiling You down to a life coach, someone I can look up to. But if You really rose from the grave, everything has to change. Today, I surrender.

WEEK 3

DOUBTS ABOUT THE BIBLE

I have a Bible near my bed.

—*President Donald Trump*

DAY 11

WHY SHOULD *ANYONE* TRUST THE BIBLE?

E ven for unbelievers, the people who wrote the Bible had some good things to say: Love your neighbor. Do unto others as you would have them do unto you. The parable of the good Samaritan. But in the minds of thoughtful agnostics and atheists, the Bible has three serious credibility issues that can't be overlooked.

First, Christians say the Bible is inerrant, but it's apparently full of contradictions.

Second, Christians act like God Himself wrote the Bible, but it was obviously written by men with their own agendas.

Third, while the Bible offers some helpful ideas, most of the good stuff (like the Golden Rule) is also found in other holy books, and there's also a lot of bad stuff (violence, sexism, and so on) that's impossible to ignore.

Many people can't understand why Christians seem to worship a book that promotes a God who exclusively loves devout believers, threatens eternal hell for bad behavior, condones slavery, condemns gays, is anti-drinking, and sex-negative. Nonbelievers wonder why Christians can't just learn from Jesus without tethering themselves to all those antiquated moral codes.

Can the Bible be trusted as an answer to life's questions? Most people under forty emphatically say no. They've heard too many Christians misusing Scripture to serve their own agendas. Their experiences are valid, and Christians better listen up.

It's also important to remember that hateful Christians who falsely represent the Bible don't falsify the Bible. They discredit themselves, not the Scriptures. It's the Jar Jar Binks principle: his appearance didn't make *Star Wars* a worthless franchise. His inclusion was unfortunate, and it never should have happened, but it doesn't change the brilliance of the original source material.

The Bible is perfect *and* messy. I can't deny some of the apparent discrepancies. I know they can be confusing, but these issues are easily explained and extraordinarily minor. You'd actually expect *more* disparities considering the Bible comprises sixty-six different books written over a thousand years by at least forty different authors.

You can interpret the Bible's trustworthiness in one of three ways. First, religious fanatics will say, "God wrote the Bible, and we know that's true because the Bible says so." This kind of bias-confirming, circular logic drives skeptics insane, but in my experience, this is exactly the way non-Christians expect Christians to interpret Scripture.

A second way some people interpret the Bible is through the lens of suspicion. Someone in this frame of mind might say, "Men with their own agendas wrote the Bible, and I know that's true because my intellect says so." This level of elitism is astounding. The cynic trusts his own intellect more than a thousand years of powerful literature, history, poetry, and parables that have changed the world and inspired countless songs, the greatest works of art, the best hospitals and universities the world has ever seen, and the pursuit of a more just society where all men are created equal. I'm sure you're pretty smart, but your singular mind is not more trustworthy than the Bible.

The third way to examine the Bible's trustworthiness is to read it as a story about God and His intentions for creation. The word *story* is key here, because stories are how people make sense of things. That's the one thing that has never changed about human beings. We've changed the way we live, what we eat, how we organize civilizations, how we get married, how we raise children, and how we choose our leaders. But "people have always told stories as they searched for Truth. As our ancient ancestors sat around the campfire in front of their caves, they told the stories of their day in order to try to understand what their day had meant, what the truth of the mammoth hunt was, or the roar of the cave lion, or the falling in love of two young people."[1]

Without stories, there's no meaning to life. When Christians say the Bible is holy, we don't mean we'll be offended if you burn it or you're not allowed to question it; we mean the sixty-six books, forty authors, and nine literary genres spanning over a thousand years tell the master narrative about God and His intentions for the world He created. It's a story about an all-powerful God who's willing to suffer and die for the same people who rejected and killed Him.

It is the Story of stories, and it is perfect in every way that counts.

Today's Scripture

"For the word of God is living and active, sharper than any two-edged sword, piercing to the division of soul and of spirit, of joints and of marrow, and discerning the thoughts and intentions of the heart. And no creature is hidden from his sight, but all are naked and exposed to the eyes of him to whom we must give account. Since then we have a great high priest who has passed through the heavens, Jesus, the Son of God, let us hold fast our confession." (Hebrews 4:12-14 ESV)

Today's Prayer

My mind is open. My heart is soft. I am ready to play my part in the story You are telling.

DAY 12

What Makes the Bible
Any Different from Other
Sacred Texts?

People have always written mythologies about their gods, and to the average person, they all look alike. All religious texts have a morality code, God (or gods) who is (or are) often angry or dissatisfied, and systems of eternal reward and punishment. It can sound arrogant to others when Christians assume the Bible is holier than other holy books because, when they read the Bible, they see a creation story that contradicts science, a tricky, talking snake, and a childish God who floods the whole earth for no good reason—and that's just the first nine chapters of the first book!

To many non-Christians, the Bible looks just like any other old book of myths, and the idea that any educated person could worship such a book in the twenty-first century is beyond comprehension. But it's important to remember that Christians don't actually *worship* the Bible. Christianity was *never* about loving a book, but a Person. We worship God; the Bible just tells His story.

The Bible obviously shares themes with other holy books—morality, hospitality, forgiveness, and so on—but saying the Bible's message is the same as all other sacred texts is intellectual malpractice. There are too many important distinctions to ignore.

First of all, no other holy book can match the Bible's *diversity*: forty authors writing on three continents in at least three languages covering ten literary genres over a thousand years' time. Most holy books, such as the Torah, the Quran, and the Book of Mormon rely on one man's secret revelation from God; the Bible relies on forty independent sources testifying to the same core truths.

The Bible's *consistency* is also remarkable. Its authors included kings, fishermen, scholars, day laborers, priests, a tax collector, a tentmaker, and two half-brothers of Jesus, and they all contributed parts of the same, seamless story of God's gracious, patient affection. From Genesis to Revelation, the Bible speaks of one God and His unbreakable love for creation.

The Bible's *historicity* is unrivaled among the world's holy books. Science and archaeology continue to affirm much of the biblical narrative. For years scholars thought Jericho was a fictional city, and then they found ruins believed to be congruent with ancient Jericho. They used to think King David was merely mythical until they uncovered evidence of his actual reign. They even thought Pontius Pilate was made up; then archaeologists discovered an ancient inscription that corroborates the biblical account.

A common criticism of the Bible is that it's been twisted by translators over time, but the Bible's *accuracy* is outstanding. There are more than five thousand ancient manuscripts of the New Testament alone, and they've been proven to match one another 99.5 percent of the time. By comparison, we have six hundred ancient manuscripts of Homer's *The Iliad*, and those manuscripts match one another only 95 percent of the time. Of course, you'll never hear a college professor question the legitimacy of *The Iliad*, but the Bible is fair game.

I love that the writers of the Bible didn't know they were writing Scripture. With the exception of the first five books of the Old Testament, the Bible's authors didn't finish their books with "This is *the* Law. Obey or die!" Unlike most other religious books, the Bible is *descriptive*, not *prescriptive*, describing events that already happened instead of prescribing a rigid dogma to obey.

Finally, the Bible's story *hinges on Jesus*. I love that Jesus throws the door wide open for people of all races and cultures to belong to one family. The Bible, which began in diversity, is the holy book for the most diverse movement the world has ever known.

Christians don't believe the Bible saves us or makes us holy; only Jesus can do that. You don't have to say, eat, or do the right thing for God to love and accept you (see Ephesians 2:8-9). Jesus said understanding God is as simple as looking at a father who is desperate for his lost child to come back home. And no matter how long you've been gone, no matter what you've done, when He sees you coming, He runs to meet you. He kisses you and throws you a party. In terms of world religions, that's really different. That's the difference Jesus makes.

More than anything else, Jesus is what makes the Bible unique.

Today's Scripture

"For God did not send his Son into the world to condemn the world, but to save the world through him." (John 3:17)

Today's Prayer

Thank You for the Bible. I'm sorry I've taken it for granted. Break my heart of stone, dissect my intellectual pride, and help me to see Your story for what it is.

DAY 13

Why Is the Old Testament God So Angry?

Most people are OK with the New Testament. Jesus seems like the kind of guy you might like to get a beer or a cup of coffee with. But in the Old Testament, God seems angry and bloodthirsty. He ordered war, genocide, capital punishment, and honor killings. He seems more archaic and tribal than Jesus, whose love-your-enemies message sounds like a major departure from the Bible before Christ.

This problem isn't new; it goes all the way back to the second century AD. Around 130, a wealthy Roman Christian named Marcion had serious problems with the violence and cruelty he found in the Old Testament. He decided Yahweh was not the true God who sent Jesus to save the world. Marcion created his own Bible with only New Testament books, and his wealthy Christian friends in Rome loved it.

But that's exactly the point: the more wealth we have, and the more comfortable we get in life, the easier it is to dismiss "Old Testament God." Most of us who live with great privilege have a reasonable expectation of justice if we're robbed or assaulted. Just call the cops and let them work it out. But there are places in the world where there's no 911. There are places where the cops are the perps, and there's no remedy and no justice. You just have to cope with reality.

That's real life for *most* people in the world today, but it was much, much worse for the Israelites three thousand years ago, when the Old Testament was being written. It was a savage world. The Egyptians devastated the economies of the local tribes. The jobless men in the region formed gangs that wandered the countryside robbing men and raping women. In ancient documents, gang leaders bragged about boring through the bodies of their enemies, creating rivers of blood, flaying the skin off of living victims in full view of their families, and cutting the genitalia off of prisoners of war—and feeding it to the victim.

There are two problems with the dualistic approach to biblical interpretation that seeks to separate Old Testament savagery from New Testament grace. First, it assumes the Old Testament God was *always* violent, but there are many examples of God's love in the Old Testament, such as Isaiah 61:1:

> The Spirit of the Sovereign Lord is on me,
>   because the Lord has anointed me
>   to proclaim good news to the poor;
> He has sent me to bind up the brokenhearted,
>   to proclaim freedom for the captives
>   and release from darkness for the
>   prisoners.

This is God's ideal world, but He also knows the real world. He gets His hands dirty. He comes and lives with us. He knows our struggle. He hates death and refuses to take it lying down, which leads to Marcion's second problem: Marcion assumed Jesus was always kind and *never* violent.

Everybody knows Jesus loved kids, right? In Matthew 18:2-5, Jesus called a little child to Him, and placed the child among him and his disciples. And he said, "Truly I tell you, unless you change and become like little children, you will never enter the kingdom of heaven. Therefore, whoever takes the lowly position of this child is the greatest in the kingdom of heaven. And whoever welcomes one such child in my name welcomes me."

That is just *so sweet*. Classic Jesus. What a nice guy! But wait, here's the very next verse: "If anyone causes one of these little ones . . . to stumble, it would be better for them to have a large millstone hung around their neck and to be drowned in the depths of the sea" (v. 6).

I did not see that coming. That's not sweet at all. Jesus sounds like a gangster straight out of *Goodfellas*.

God hates violence, but there are things He hates more than violence, like being separated from His kids. That's what most of the hard-to-read parts of the Bible are really about.

Dr. Martin Luther King Jr. put it this way: "At times we need to know that the Lord is a God of justice. . . . When our most tireless efforts fail to stop the surging sweep of oppression, we need to know that in this universe is a God whose matchless strength is a fit contrast to the sordid weakness of man."[2]

The point of being a Christian isn't that you never get violent and fight. It's *how* you fight that counts, who you're fighting *for*, and what you're fighting *against*. God's heart still burns hot with rage when anybody or anything messes with His kids, and our hearts should, too.

Today's Scripture

"Give ear and come to me; listen, that you may live." (Isaiah 55:3)

Today's Prayer

Help me to fight, to wage war on the forces of darkness at work in my own life, in my home, in my city, and in Your world today.

DAY 14

Why Is the Bible So Hard to Understand? (Part 1)

I like to think I'm a smart guy. I've read a dozen novels by Dostoevsky and Tolstoy. I once completed a *New York Times* crossword puzzle in under ninety minutes. I'm the guy my friends call when they're watching mind-bending movies like *Interstellar* and have no idea what's going on. I can comprehend just about anything I read, but the Bible never fails to confuse me.

Allow me to offer a few examples:

> Exodus 4:24-26: "At a lodging place on the way, the LORD met Moses and was about to kill him. But Zipporah took a flint knife, cut off her son's foreskin and touched Moses' feet with it. 'Surely you are a bridegroom of blood to me,' she said. So the LORD let him alone."

So. Many. Questions.

> Numbers 22:27-30: "When the donkey saw the angel of the LORD, it lay down under Balaam, and he was angry and beat it with his staff. Then the LORD opened the donkey's mouth, and it said to Balaam, 'What have I done to you to make you beat me these three times?' Balaam answered the donkey, 'You have made a fool of me! If only I had a sword in my hand, I would kill you right now.' The donkey said to Balaam, 'Am I not your own

donkey, which you have always ridden, to this day? Have I been in the habit of doing this to you?'"

We're believing in talking donkeys now?

Ephesians 6:5: "Slaves, obey your earthly masters with respect and fear, and with sincerity of heart, just as you would obey Christ."

Gulp

But as a fan of Dostoevsky, I must acknowledge the importance of context. His masterpiece, *The Brothers Karamazov*, is clearly inspired by the time he spent doing hard time in prison and fighting in the Russian military. The most famous scene in that book—the courtroom—was shaped by his own time standing in front of the judge. You can't understand Dostoevsky, or any author, unless you know where he's coming from.

Many secularists today are happy to write the Bible off as nonsense without first doing their homework to understand its context. Before dismissing something as archaic, you should at least find out where it comes from, who wrote it, and why. I've heard scholars criticize the Old Testament law to take an "eye for an eye" (Leviticus 24:20), suggesting it condones retributive, vigilante justice. But taken in context, an "eye for an eye" represented a sharp, progressive approach to righting wrongs. Three thousand years ago, when someone stole from your tribe, you stole twice as much from theirs—or you cut off their arms, or you killed them. An "eye for an eye" was the most forward-thinking law of the land, contextually speaking.

The passage about slaves and masters is another example of the importance of context. I'm sure everyone would love for the apostle Paul in the New Testament to have said, "Masters, free your slaves," but that's imposing our twenty-first-century, Western, enlightened will onto a foreign, minority culture (which, by the way, is something intellectual humanists tend to find repulsive). Paul's mission was to make it possible for slaves and servants to participate in the churches and to hear the gospel of Jesus Christ. Whenever you read Ephesians 6:5, don't stop reading before you get to verse 9: "Slaves, obey your earthly masters with respect and fear, and with sincerity of heart, just as you would obey Christ.... And masters, *treat your slaves the same way*. Do not threaten them, since you know that he who is both their Master and yours is in heaven, and there is no favoritism with him" (Ephesians 6:5, 9 emphasis added).

Paul knew very well that requiring all masters to free their slaves would, at best, achieve freedom for a few. But if masters and slaves heard the gospel together, it would be the beginning of a movement that would free millions of slaves in the coming years.

Don't ever tell me the Bible isn't radically relevant and revolutionary; it has enjoyed its unprecedented shelf life for a reason. You *can* understand it. You *can* trust it. The Bible is the story of God, inspired by God, for the people of God.

Now, about that donkey...we'll start there tomorrow.

Today's Scripture

"The grass withers, the flower fades, But the word of our God stands forever." (Isaiah 40:8)

Today's Prayer

I want to know Your story better for myself, Jesus. Give me the courage to start each day with Your Word. Thank You.

DAY 15

Why Is the Bible So Hard to Understand? (Part 2)

I recognize I can't get away with saying, "It's the Word of God" on the one hand and, "All the violent, sexist stuff is just context" on the other. Obviously context matters, but at the end of the day, the Bible is either true or it isn't. And that applies to *all* the Bible, not just the nice, sensible parts we like.

Either there really was a talking donkey, or there wasn't. Either God regretted making human beings (see Genesis 6:6-8), or He didn't. Either God really sanctioned the deaths of children (see Hosea 13:16), or it would appear the Bible is false. And if the Bible is false, the Christian faith is worthless. To many outside the church, the Bible looks like fiction: fun to read at times, but not worthy of our allegiance.

Context matters, but it's not all that matters when reading the Bible. There's something else that is equally important: genre. The Bible isn't just one book written at one time from a single point of view; it's more like a library containing several literary genres. Calling the Bible "fiction" is like calling a library "fiction"; it doesn't make sense.

People (including Christians) are prone to talk about the Bible like it's a monolithic document; we say things like "The Bible says..." when it wouldn't make sense to say "The Library says...." When studying or critiquing the Bible, we must be aware that it comprises at least ten genres (listed here with examples of Bible books that belong in each category):

law (Leviticus, Deuteronomy)
history (Joshua, Acts)
prophecy (Isaiah, Micah)
poetry (Genesis 1, Job)
wisdom (Proverbs, Ecclesiastes)
music (Psalms, Song of Songs)
romance (Song of Songs, Ruth)
biography (Genesis 12–50, the four Gospels—
    Matthew, Mark, Luke, and John)
correspondence (Romans, 2 Peter)
apocalyptic (Revelation, Daniel)

Many critics of the Bible suffer from genre confusion, which can get messy in a hurry. In 1938, a CBS Radio broadcast celebrated Halloween by reading a live adaptation of H. G. Wells's novel *The War of the Worlds*, an alien-invasion thriller. Not enough people were listening at the beginning, when the performance was introduced, and by intermission America was freaking out. Police were on high alert. Men loaded their guns. Children wept in fear.

It was a cruel prank, given the context—in 1938, with half the world already at war, Hitler advanced toward Poland, and the Third Reich established the first concentration camp. *The War of the Worlds* broadcast capitalized on the fears that already held many Americans hostage. But it all came down to genre: the people interpreted a mystery-thriller as though it was a news broadcast.

The same thing happens with Scripture. Some parts of the Bible were written as history: Luke's Gospel begins with "I...decided to write an orderly account for you...so that you may know the certainty of the things you have been taught" (vv. 3-4). This is a clear indication that Luke intended for what followed to be interpreted literally.

Other parts of the Bible are part history, part theology. Think Noah and the Flood or Samson and his hair. These writings were never meant to be read like news reports; they're framing actual, historical events through the lens of God and His concern for His people.

Some of the most horrific parts of Scripture are found in the Psalms. The Psalms were songs people sang, and many of those songs were written and sung during times of war, famine, and disease. Music is how humans express our deepest fears and emotions, and we see that angst coming through in some of the Bible's darkest verses. Read the Psalms like they're the songs of a starving, war-torn minority, and things may get a little clearer.

For me, the human element doesn't take away from the Bible's truth; it adds authenticity to Scripture. The Bible is a real collection of books about real human life and a real God who cares enough to intervene when we're at our worst.

Figuring out context and genre will clear most of the hurdles people face when getting acquainted with the Bible. You simply have to know what you're reading.

Doubts about the Bible can be good, but at some point you have to decide what to *do* about your doubts. I hope you won't let what you've heard about the Bible keep you from diving in headfirst and seeing for yourself.

Today's Scripture

"When you pass through the waters, I will be with you; and when you pass through the rivers, they will not sweep over you. When you walk through the fire, you will not be burned.... For I am the LORD your

God....Since you are precious and honored in my sight, and because I love you...Do not be afraid, for I am with you." (Isaiah 43:2-5)

Today's Prayer

I've been stuck in my doubts for too long. I want to take a leap of faith. I trust that You'll be there to help me understand Your Word. Thank You.

WEEK 4

Doubts About the
Human Condition

A lot of what is most beautiful about the world arises from struggle.

—Malcolm Gladwell

DAY 16

How Do You Explain Pain?

You don't need to know evolutionary biology and quantum mechanics to be an atheist; just take a look around and you'll see why belief in God—especially a loving God—can feel like a waste of time. Look how many kids are being raised in poverty. Think about the mother of three who got cancer and died in her thirties. Every day, over 120 Americans take their own lives. How miserable a place must this world be if so many people simply want out?

All the while, God seems to keep His distance, remaining silent. To many people who are struggling, it seems like God either doesn't exist, or He doesn't care. I'm not sure which would be worse.

Every Sunday morning when I stand up to teach, I look out at a sea of people covered in scars:

- emotionally scarred young adults who had (or have) abusive parents;
- a man in his forties who was hurt while trying to escape the South Tower on 9/11;
- a woman in her sixties who, thirty years ago, fell asleep at the wheel and crashed, killing four of her five kids;
- a woman in her twenties who, six weeks after her dream wedding, discovered her husband is physically abusive.

While I agree it's sometimes hard to comprehend why a loving God would allow so many people to suffer, I have to ask three questions:

> 1. What should we expect from a loving God?
> 2. What's the alternative?
> 3. And is it worth it?

Consider this: if God is real, and if God is love, *what kind of world should we expect Him to make?*

Love can't be coerced, enforced, shamed, or controlled; it must be freely chosen. So if a loving God created us for love, then we should expect to have the freedom to choose love, or to choose fear, isolation, self-interest, violence, and oppression—all of which sound like the root causes of our pain.

What's the alternative to a loving God? What if God prioritized painlessness over love? The alternative to a God of love and freedom would be a supreme micromanager who seeks to control people by means of reward and punishment. Sadly, that's the image of God that some Christians project to those outside the church. But God's true nature, according to Jesus and the Bible, is love.

That's an insufficient explanation for people whose wounds are just too deep. The question they're asking is, Why would a loving God subject us to a world so prone to pain and loss? It's a great question. If it's really all about love, *is love worth the risk?*

We know the answer.

Why give your heart to another human being, if they might break it? Why get married, if you might get divorced? Why have kids, if they might suffer? Because we know, deep down, that the potential for real love is always worth the risk of pain and loss.

Today's Scripture

"And after you have suffered a little while, the God of all grace, who has called you to his eternal glory in Christ, will himself restore, confirm, strengthen, and establish you." (1 Peter 5:10 ESV)

Today's Prayer

I pray for those in pain, for those who are all alone in the world, for children who are afraid, for those who are sick and tired, for those who are stressed out, for those who just want their life to end. However possible, according to Your will, I pray You will use me to ease someone's pain.

DAY 17

WILL GOD REALLY NEVER GIVE YOU MORE THAN YOU CAN HANDLE?

My friend Philip was the guy every guy wanted to be, and the guy every girl wanted to be with. He was 6'3", athletic, smart, and funny. He was also one of my best friends. We grew up together in the same small town; we were baptized at the same country church. We played on the same baseball team for most of our childhood.

Then, in the blink of an eye, Philip was gone. On July 31, 1995, he turned his Chevy pickup in front of an eighteen wheeler, and he was instantly killed. Our tiny, tight-knit community was in shock; within hours we all converged on Philip's house to comfort his family. I was sixteen, and I'll never forget standing in the garage with Philip's dad and brother as they tightly hugged pictures of Philip and sobbed.

A local preacher tried to comfort Philip's dad by saying, "I guess heaven's team needed a good third baseman." Then he asked us to hold hands as he led us in prayer. He said something like, "We don't understand why things like this happen, Lord, but your word promises us you will never give us more than we can handle."

I can't imagine how those words must have sounded to Philip's dad, who rarely stepped foot in a church again after that day. Losing a child is more than anyone can handle, and that happens every day. When Christians say things like "God will never give you more than you can handle," it feels condescending and dismissive to those who have been utterly broken by the hand they've been dealt.

There are two things to remember about that phrase. First, it's taken out of context. "God will never give you more than you can handle" is rooted in 1 Corinthians 10:13, where Paul is clearly talking about temptation and sin, not pain and loss: "No temptation has overtaken you that is not common to man. God is faithful, and he will not let you be tempted beyond your ability, but with the temptation he will also provide the way of escape, that you may be able to endure it."

Second, we need to deal with the assumption that God "gives" us everything that comes our way. Some Christians talk as if everything that happens in the world *must* be God's will, but not even Jesus believed that. That's why he taught us to pray for God's will to "be done, on earth as it is in heaven" (Matthew 6:11). If it was a given, we wouldn't need to pray for it.

Some things that happen to people are not the will of God. Some things that have happened to you were not the will of God. And sometimes it's way more than we can handle.

God's promise isn't to be the Almighty Helicopter Parent who protects you from every awful thing. Instead, when it all falls apart:

- God comes near to you. "The Lord is close to the brokenhearted and saves those who are crushed in spirit" (Psalm 34:18). He doesn't wait for you to get it together. He doesn't wait for you to get back in church. He finds you in the darkest places to help show you the way out.

- God grows your character. "Not only so, but we also glory in our sufferings, because we know that suffering produces perseverance; perseverance, character; and character, hope" (Romans 5:3-4). God will take something that wasn't His will for your life and turn it around for good. He will use your pain to make you stronger, and as you recover, he will give you opportunities to help others who are going through something similar to what you've been through.

- God restores you. "The God of all grace, who called you to his eternal glory in Christ, after you have suffered a little while, will himself restore you and make you strong, firm and steadfast" (1 Peter 5:10). As you heal, God will strengthen and establish you, giving you the courage to shed the victim mentality that often keeps people in darkness.

You may not believe it now, but there will soon be a time when you will look back on your worst day and see how God was with you all along.

Today's Scripture

"The LORD is close to the brokenhearted and saves those who are crushed in spirit." (Psalm 34:18)

Today's Prayer

Our Father in heaven,
Hallowed be Your name.
Your kingdom come.
Your will be done
On earth as *it is* in heaven.
Give us this day our daily bread.
And forgive us our debts,

As we forgive our debtors.
And do not lead us into temptation,
But deliver us from the evil one.
For Yours is the kingdom and the power and the glory forever.
Amen. (Matthew 6:9-13 NKJV)

DAY 18

WHAT GOOD DOES PRAYER DO?

I know prayer can help people better themselves. It has been shown to increase focus and concentration in the classroom and the office. Prayer can be a tool that makes us sharper and more productive.

But many people think prayer is just about believers pleading with God to do something He wasn't already planning to do. And to many nonreligious folks, that sounds utterly ridiculous. They can't fathom how someone with any level of education would sit and talk to an invisible spirit in the sky, rattling off a wish list like it's Christmas and He's the Almighty Santa Claus.

When I was in seminary, I stopped asking God for stuff. I got too smart, I guess. Asking God for stuff felt shallow. I mean, nobody really believes indigenous people caused it to rain by dancing in a circle around a fire, do they? But what's the difference between them doing a rain dance and me begging God for the new Apple Watch?

This was my line of thinking: if God is all-knowing, He already knows what I want, what I need, and whether I'm going to get it. If God is all-powerful, He's able to do whatever He wants regardless of my prayers (or lack thereof). And if God is all-good, He's going to look out for me, whether or not I'm on my knees begging for help. Otherwise, one of three things is true: God isn't real, God doesn't care, or God is like a playground bully who makes you say His name before letting you up off the ground. If God is God, I figured, what's the point of praying for stuff?

I realize I'm not alone in my skepticism. Many intellectual believers have decided that meditation, contemplation, and practicing mindfulness are higher forms of prayer than asking God for things. These practices may be worthwhile supplements to prayer, but they're certainly not suitable substitutes. Prayer is the conversation, the communication, the speaking and the listening with God. But some heady Christians are no longer asking God for things because they simply don't think it works. To them, praying for something specific seems like "a spasm of words lost in a cosmic indifference."[1]

Sometimes I'd rather just pray in silence, drink coffee, maybe write a few notes or read a good book. Rather than just speaking into the uncertainty of thin air, I prefer to stay in control of my life and use my time wisely.

The only trouble, of course, is that while a little peace and quiet, self-reflection, coffee, and a good book may sound like heaven, it doesn't sound much like *prayer*.

Prayer is defined by who is at the center. If your "prayer" is all about self-improvement and making *you* more productive, it's probably not prayer, because *you* are at the center of it. Which makes *you* God. And you're not God.

You know that, right?

Please tell me you know that.

The first purpose of prayer is to realign your perspective about the universe, namely the fact that you are not the center of it. Prayer begins by putting God where only He belongs. When you do that, two things will happen: first, you'll be wonderstruck by the immensity of God's creation. Second, you'll be humbled by the privilege of bending God's ear in prayer. Like King David, you'll find yourself thinking,

> When I consider Your heavens, the work of Your
>   fingers,

> The moon and the stars, which you have
>   ordained,
> what is man that You are mindful of him?
>   (Psalm 8:3-4 NKJV)

My journey back from intellectual materialism toward supernatural faith has led me to ask new questions about prayer: What if, when we say things like, "If God is good, He'll give me what I need without me begging Him for it," we have prayer backward? What if we looked at prayer this way instead: "Because God is good, He inspires us to be actors in the story He is writing"?

I'm sure God's will for me involves my not dying of dehydration, but I still have to act, right? I'm the one who has to drink the water? Also, I'm fairly certain God intends for my kids to eat breakfast when they wake up, but He won't be the one standing over the waffle iron an hour from now, will He? Furthermore, I believe God's desire is for me to be a friend to the woman who sleeps on the sidewalk up the street from my house, but God isn't going to force me to tell her my name, is He?

What if God has already written the outline of eternity's script, but daily, He leaves room in the narrative for us to improvise? What if prayer is improvisation? What if prayer is me accepting my role in the greatest story ever told, and doing whatever I can to make it even better?

Philosopher Blaise Pascal said, "God instituted prayer in order to lend to His creatures the dignity of causality."[2] I don't know *how*, I just know prayer changes things. It changes me. It changes other people. It can even influence the Author to alter a page in His story.

The arrogant cynic may say, as I used to, "It's foolish and quaint to ask God for things," while day after day, the foolish faithful get on their knees and change the world.

Today's Scripture

"Do not be anxious about anything, but in every situation, by prayer and petition, with thanksgiving, present your requests to God."

(Philippians 4:6)

Today's Prayer

Lord, make me an instrument of your peace.
Where there is hatred, let me sow love;
where there is injury, pardon;
where there is doubt, faith;
where there is despair, hope;
where there is darkness, light;
where there is sadness, joy.
O divine Master, grant that I may not so much seek
to be consoled as to console,
to be understood as to understand,
to be loved as to love.
For it is in giving that we receive,
it is in pardoning that we are pardoned,
and it is in dying that we are born to eternal life.
Amen.
(Peace Prayer of Saint Francis)

DAY 19

WHY DOES GOD PUNISH SINNERS?

Many people think it's just a cruel experiment conducted by a power-hungry bully/dictator and the men in leadership around him. No, I don't mean the federal government (#heyooo)—I'm talking about God and the church and why Christian leaders seem to be so fixated on punishing sinners. Why does God want to punish people, and why do some Christians seem so giddy when talking about the damnation of those outside the church?

Have you ever seen one of those "confessional box" scenes in a movie? Those scenes make me cringe every time. Like most bad ideas, the confessional began with the best of intentions; in the sixteenth century, the Catholic Church began offering believers a private, anonymous place to confess their sins to a priest. But soon enough, it became a pay-to-pray system, and now, for many outside the church, the confessional is a symbol of religious corruption. They imagine it working something like this:

> **Sinner:** "Holy Father, I got drunk, went to my neighbor's house, and spray painted his cat."
> **Priest:** "Oh, my. Say three 'Our Fathers' and seven 'Hail Marys,' and you will be forgiven."
> **Sinner:** "I should mention that while I was there, I also slept with my neighbor's wife."
> **Priest:** "That's gonna cost you another 'Hail Mary.'"

Confession is biblical, but it's not supposed to be a game by which you escape God's wrath. Like any intimate relationship, your connection to God depends on honesty and transparency. Confession is the believer's way of saying, "Something's not right here," and allowing God to wipe the slate clean. First John 1:9 says, "If we confess our sins, he is faithful and just to forgive us our sins and to cleanse us from all unrighteousness."

But what happens when we don't come clean with God? Well, the same thing that happens when we don't come clean in any relationship: more covering your tracks, less intimacy, more distance between you and the other person. And one day, that distance crosses the point of no return, and there's no more connection between you and the other person. Whenever that happens with you and God, that's hell.

Jesus told a story about a rich man and the beggar, Lazarus, who lived outside the gate to the rich man's house. Both men die, and Lazarus goes to heaven while the rich man goes to hell. The rich man looks up and sees the beggar in heaven, standing next to the Old Testament patriarch, Abraham. Jesus said, "So he called to him, 'Father Abraham, have pity on me and send Lazarus to dip the tip of his finger in water and cool my tongue, because I am in agony in this fire.' But Abraham replied, 'Son, remember that in your lifetime you received your good things, while Lazarus received bad things, but now he is comforted here and you are in agony'" (Luke 16:24-31).

Even though he's in hell, the rich man is oblivious. He still expects a poor beggar like Lazarus to be his water boy. He doesn't get to heaven; he wants a servant boy to come serve him in hell. Later in the story, he blames God for his fate; he says he wasn't given enough information. And you probably noticed that, while Lazarus is just a beggar, he's called by name in Jesus's story, but the rich man isn't, because his whole identity is wrapped up in getting his hands on more money.

I'm not sure God ever sent a single person to hell; it seems to me the punishment for sins is self-inflicted. It's a choice, and it happens slowly, you know? Like an addiction. First, there's something you like. Then you love it and you need more and more of it. You get lost in your desire for it. The people who care for you call you out on it, and you blame them for not understanding you, for being against you. They are the problem. Then it—whatever it is—is your daddy. It becomes your god. It owns you, and you might as well not even have a name, because your entire identity is wrapped up in your insatiable need to possess the object of your addiction.

C. S. Lewis said:

> Hell begins with a grumbling mood, always complaining, always blaming others...but you are still distinct from it. You may even criticize it in yourself and wish you could stop it. But there may come a day when you can no longer. Then there will be no "you" left to criticize the mood or even to enjoy it, but just the grumble itself, going on forever like a machine. It is not a question of God "sending us" to hell. In each of us there is something growing, which will BE hell unless it's taken care of.... There are only two kinds of people—those who say "Thy will be done" to God or those to whom God says in the end, "Thy will be done." All that are in hell choose it. Without that self-choice it wouldn't be hell. No soul that seriously and constantly desires joy will ever miss it.[3]

God doesn't want you to miss the joy of being forgiven, but He's committed to giving you the freedom to choose it, or not to. You don't need a priest, or a confessional box, or any number of Hail Marys. You just need Jesus, the slightest bit of self-awareness, and the courage to say, "I believe."

Today's Scripture

"When you were dead in your sins...God made you alive with Christ. He forgave us all our sins, having canceled the charge of our legal indebtedness....He has taken it away, nailing it to the cross. And having disarmed the powers and authorities, and made a public spectacle of them, triumphing over them." (Colossians 2:13-15)

Today's Prayer

Forgive me. Thank You. I love You.

DAY 20

Is It a Sin to Have Doubts?

When I was sixteen I went to an amusement park, Six Flags Over Texas in Dallas, with a group from my church because it was Christian Family Day, and they were planning to host a big Christian concert that night. I had a great day filled with roller coasters and flirting with girls, and then came time for the concert in the outdoor amphitheater. There were a couple of opening acts, and then the headliner: Gospel Music Hall of Famer Twila Paris.

By the time she took the stage, it was dark, and we were up on a hill, so we could see for miles. I saw lightning in the distance, coming closer by the minute. Soon we were hearing thunder, too. The wind picked up, and then came the rain. Twila and her band left the stage once, but before her audience left, Twila ran back out like a boss and offered to play one more song—her most famous hit called "God Is in Control."

The crowd went nuts. Twila screamed into the mic, "I know it's ugly out here, but I know this song is true, and we know God will hold back this storm and let us worship Him!" And the people were so happy. That was the first time I ever remember looking at a bunch of Christians and thinking, "I'm not like these people." I loved God and Twila as much as the next guy, but I knew a funnel cloud when I saw one.

And sure enough, halfway through "God Is in Control," the wind got crazy, the power went out, the band rushed offstage. I got up and ran as fast as I could toward the parking lot. By the time I reached the church van, a tornado had touched down less than a mile away. Water came up past my ankles, and hail fell from the sky.

Ever since that night I've thought twice before saying something like, "God is in control." Whenever I hear Christians say something like that, I can't help thinking about the tornado that interrupted Twila, and about people who are going through some real-life storms of their own. How does "God is in control" sound to someone who's lonely, or someone who's lost a child, or a couple who can't get pregnant? If God is in control of your awful, painful circumstances, what does that say about God?

I remember the ride home on that church van; it might have been the first time I ever doubted God. I wondered then if my doubts made me a sinner, and since that night, I've met hundreds of others who sit on the fence of faith and wonder the same.

Christians have to be careful when we say things like "God is in control" because we might be misrepresenting God. When someone who has doubts about God gets the impression that being a Christian means having all the answers and never doubting Him, that person may also get the impression they don't belong with Jesus because they can't reconcile their real-life experiences with a loving God who is always in control.

The fact is, we Christians come from a long line of doubters. All the great biblical heroes had their doubts. And that includes Jesus, who wasn't always so sure about that whole crucifixion plan (Luke 22:42). What makes the people in the Bible heroes isn't just what they did; it's that in spite of their doubts, they did it anyway. Noah doubted, but he still built the ark (Genesis 6:11-22). Abraham doubted, but he still left his father's house and meandered into the desert to meet God (Genesis 12:1-4). Moses doubted, but he still stood up to Pharaoh (Exodus 3). Mary doubted, but she still said, "I am the Lord's servant.... May your word to me be fulfilled" (Luke 1:38). Sarah doubted, but she still tried to get pregnant—even though she was ninety, and her husband was a hundred (Genesis 21:1-5). Regardless of your religious orientation, we can all agree that's a noble effort.

You can doubt and be a Christian. The question for Christians isn't whether or not you have doubts; it's what you do with your doubt that counts. Yann Martel writes in *The Life of Pi*, "If Christ spent an anguished night in prayer, if he burst out from the cross, *My God, why have you forsaken me?* then surely we are permitted to doubt. But we must move on. To choose doubt as a philosophy of life is akin to choosing immobility as a means of transportation."[4]

It's OK to say we don't understand everything that happens in the world. We don't know why bad things happen to good people or why tornadoes interrupt Christian concerts. It doesn't water down our faith to say "We don't know," because faith isn't about having all the answers. It's OK to doubt, but it's toxic to let your doubts paralyze you. Faith isn't the absence of doubt; it is having some doubts, and following Jesus anyway.

Today's Scripture

"Trust in the LORD with all your heart and lean not on your own understanding; in all your ways submit to him, and he will make your paths straight." (Proverbs 3:5-6)

"Jesus said to him, 'If you can believe, all things *are* possible to him who believes.' Immediately the father of the child cried out and said with tears, 'Lord, I believe; help my unbelief!' " (Mark 9:23-24 NKJV)

Today's Prayer

My doubts are a catalyst launching me toward Your Truth. When I lack courage, give me strength to continue along the journey to wisdom and understanding. Thank You.

WEEK 5

DOUBTS ABOUT
FAITH AND SCIENCE

Is it hot in here? I'm sweating like a Christian in science class!

—Anonymous

DAY 21

WHAT IF THOMAS JEFFERSON WAS RIGHT?

Just about everyone agrees that Jesus was a remarkable man. His teachings are timeless; He inspired a movement that undeniably changed the world. But that doesn't make him God, does it? Thomas Jefferson deeply admired Jesus but rejected the religion that bore His name. Writing to William Short, Jefferson insisted, "Jesus did not mean to impose himself on mankind as the Son of God."[1]

Jefferson believed Jesus's disciples, with the help of the apostle Paul—whom Jefferson called "the first corrupter of the doctrines of Jesus"—were "ignorant, unlettered men" guilty of producing "superstitions, fanaticisms, and fabrications" after Jesus's death. He believed they took a gifted moral teacher and made a god out of Jesus, built a religion around Him, and made themselves rich and famous because of Him.

So Jefferson took a razor blade to his Bible, cutting out all things miraculous and supernatural—from the story of Jesus's birth to His miracles and resurrection. What remained were His sermons and parables, which Jefferson glued together and bound in a new gospel he coined "The Life and Morals of Jesus of Nazareth."[2]

What if doubting Thomas Jefferson was right? What if Jesus was just an extraordinary teacher and His followers didn't want to let Him die, so they made Him their god?

Jefferson was an enigma. In some ways he was about two centuries ahead of his time, and he might have felt more at home in the twenty-first century than the eighteenth. He believed in God, but hated organized religion. He loved Jesus, but despised religious leaders. He fawned over rock star scientists—modern-day versions of Bill Nye and Neil deGrasse Tyson—once calling Newton, Bacon, and Locke "the three greatest men who ever lived."[3]

But Jefferson was also a walking contradiction. He spent his life swearing by the principles of individual freedom and the abolition of slavery while holding six hundred slaves of his own. He renounced organized religion as a tool used to manipulate the masses, and then, as president, he encouraged priests and missionaries to evangelize Native Americans because he knew it would be much easier to coerce the Natives to submit to the white man's westward expansion once they surrendered to the white man's Western religion.

When I consider "The Life and Morals of Jesus of Nazareth," I'm not surprised to learn of Jefferson's conflicting interests. Cutting and pasting your own gospel together based on whatever makes you comfortable requires an extraordinary tolerance for contradiction.

When it comes to Jesus, people today are just as conflicted. Ninety percent of Americans think highly of Jesus, but only 40 percent claim to be deeply devoted to Him, and only 20 percent worship Him on a weekly basis. The overwhelming majority of us like Jesus, but few of us love Him, follow Him, and make disciples for Him.

Like Thomas Jefferson, people today prefer to approve of Jesus's morality while essentially rejecting his claims of divinity. More people than ever want to say, "I like what Jesus had to say, but all the other stuff—the miracles and the resurrection—I just don't buy it."

But you can't have it both ways. Separating Jesus's teachings from His divinity would be logical suicide because His teachings and His claims of divinity come from the same source: the New Testament. And Jesus didn't write the New Testament; His disciples and their friends did. Therefore, it's irrational to say, "Jesus's teachings are awesome," and in your next breath to say, "The men who wrote the Gospels were corrupt and dishonest!" How do you imagine we have Jesus's teachings? Who do you imagine wrote them down? You can deem the disciples trustworthy and accept their claims about Jesus as truth, or you can call them liars and reject their claims about Jesus altogether, but you can't have it both ways.

There is no such thing as Jesus the really great guy. If you believe in Jesus's words, the only logical end will find you on your knees, worshipping Him. If you don't, that's OK—but please don't cherry-pick your favorite Jesus quotes as if they're true. Because if He's not God, He's an absolute fraud.

It comes down to plausibility. Ask yourself these questions: what's more likely—that the most influential man in history was a charlatan, or that He is the Truth? What's more credible—that eleven uneducated peasants (ten of whom were crucified, beheaded, or burned alive) legitimately believed Jesus was the Son of God, or that they were so hungry for power and fame that they made it all up? What's more reasonable to believe—that those eleven Jewish guys turned into 2.3 billion people worshipping Jesus in every nation and in every language on earth because His story is true, or that those eleven guys pulled a fast one that, two thousand years later, continues to fool one-third of the global population?

In light of all the evidence, I choose to believe Jesus is who He said He is: the eternal God who, like a desperate father, approached His kids on their turf, desperate for them to know how much He loves them.

Today's Scripture

"Again the high priest asked him, 'Are you the Messiah, the Son of the Blessed One?' 'I am,' said Jesus. 'And you will see the Son of Man sitting at the right hand of the Mighty One and coming on the clouds of heaven.' The high priest tore his clothes. 'Why do we need any more witnesses?' he asked. 'You have heard the blasphemy! What do you think?' They all condemned him as worthy of death. Then some began to spit at him; they blindfolded him, struck him . . . the guards took him and beat him."

(Mark 14:61-65)

Today's Prayer

I still have questions, but today, I choose to consider the possibility that Your Gospel is entirely true. I need You to be my center today.

DAY 22

MIRACLES? REALLY?

It's been said that no rational person can be a Christian, and here's why: when you're a Christian, you have no choice but to believe in miracles. Miracles are, by definition, irrational; they require the suspension of the laws of physics, which just can't happen.

Sometimes when I hear someone say, "It's a miracle!" I have to bite my skeptical tongue. You couldn't bear children, but now you're pregnant with twins? That's great, but it's not technically a miracle. The IVF treatments worked. You narrowly avoided a head-on collision? You've got good instincts, or you were lucky. You flew on a major American airline with a pet and you both made it home unscathed? OK—you got me. Miracles do exist!

Everything that happens in the universe seems to have a natural explanation, and if scientists haven't found it yet, they probably will one day. But there is no explaining the virgin birth or turning water into wine or coming back from the dead. So how can any sensible person believe in miracles?

It's a common assumption that Christians believe in miracles because our dogma insists we must, while intellectuals don't believe in the miraculous because they're free to think for themselves. But is that really the case? Who's locked into their dogma here? Christians who consider humanity's historic, near-universal belief in miracles worthy of our attention, or atheists who insist that what we can observe is all that matters, and all that is?

The late astronomer Carl Sagan, an outspoken fan of Thomas

Jefferson's "bible," once said, "The Cosmos is all there is or ever was or ever will be."[4] Look closely at that quote: Sagan didn't just say the Cosmos is all we know about; he said the Cosmos is all there is and all there ever will be.

How can anyone—much less a noted scientist—make such a broad claim while offering no evidentiary support? It's one thing to say, "Science can only observe the natural world" but it's quite another to say, "The natural world is all there is."

I understand why it's hard for people to believe in miracles; many people say they've never seen one. Even if they are real, miracles seem to be rare to the point of irrelevance.

I suppose if your understanding of a miracle is something so extraordinary that it leaves you breathless, then these events are indeed very rare. But for me, the question begins and ends with the most shocking miracles of all: existence, life, and intelligence.

Science can tell us all about the Big Bang, but what about the prerequisite conditions that made it possible? Or the reasons why anything exists at all? And what of the unthinkable odds against the possibility of the emergence of life? In 2004, the renowned British philosopher and prominent atheist Anthony Flew shocked the world by "coming out" as a believer in God. Pay special attention to the rational reasons on which he based his decision:

> I now believe that the universe was brought into existence by an infinite Intelligence. I believe that this universe's intricate laws manifest what scientists have called the Mind of God. I believe that life and reproduction originate in a divine Source ... this is the world picture as I see it, that has emerged from modern science. Science spotlights three dimensions of nature that point to God. The first is the fact that

nature obeys laws. The second is the dimension of life, of intelligently organized and purpose-driven beings, which arose from matter. The third is the very existence of nature.[5]

Ralph Waldo Emerson said, "The invariable mark of wisdom is to see the miraculous in the common." After years of doubting the supernatural, I'm confident that believing in miracles is more rational than not. Existence itself is supernatural. Life is miraculous. You are a miracle, so live accordingly today.

Today's Scripture

"You *are* the God who does wonders; You have declared Your strength among the peoples." (Psalm 77:14 NKJV)

Today's Prayer

I pray for the wisdom to see the miracles right in front of me today.

DAY 23

Isn't Christianity
Anti-Intellectual?

Theoretical physicist and militant atheist Dr. Lawrence Krauss, author of the article "All Scientists Should Be Militant Atheists," was asked during a public debate whether there's anything that could ever make him believe in God. He said, "Yes, any empirical evidence whatsoever, because there is none."[6]

That reminds me of the day I decided to leave Christianity. It was my junior year of college, and my religion professor, whose anti-Christian bent was almost as vitriolic and condescending as Dr. Krauss's, strolled into class wearing a black T-shirt that read "Christianity: The belief that a Cosmic Jewish zombie who was his own father can make you live forever in his cloud kingdom if you telepathically accept him as your master and symbolically devour his flesh and so he can remove an evil force from your soul which is there because a rib-woman was convinced by a talking snake to eat from a magical tree. *Makes perfect sense.*"

Above the sound of my fellow students' laughter, the most brilliant intellectual I'd ever known proceeded to verbally eviscerate my most basic Christian beliefs. I left Christianity behind that day because I didn't want to anchor my life to something so foolish anymore. I wanted to be an intellectual, but I came to believe that you can't be academic *and* Christian. You have to choose between proven facts and blind faith.

It's *really* hard to believe much of the stuff Christians believe. God and Satan. Angels and demons. Light and darkness. Sin and salvation.

Death and resurrection. Heroes and villains. It all sounds too much like *Star Wars* or *The Lord of the Rings* to be true, right? But what if I told you the producer of *Star Wars IV, V,* and *VI* (you know, the *real Star Wars* films) once said The Force was a representation of the Holy Spirit's power in the New Testament? And what if I told you George Lucas, the creator of the *Star Wars* franchise, is a Methodist and has admitted that the popular phrase "The Force be with you" was intentionally similar to the ancient Christian greeting, "The Lord be with you" (which explains why Catholics, Episcopalians, and Methodists who hear "The Force be with you" instinctively reply "And also with you")? And what if J. R. R. Tolkien (a devout Catholic) intentionally wrote major Christian themes into *The Hobbit* and *The Lord of the Rings* trilogy?

If you don't accept the Christian worldview, that's fine. But what *do* you believe? It's easy to pick Christianity apart, but what's the alternative? Intellectuals are prone to explain the universe using only empirical, lab-tested data. At first it feels safe and comfy to know the world can be understood and there's no God to whom we're all accountable. But at the end of that line of thought is always the stark reality that nothing matters. The most famous atheist in the world, Richard Dawkins, is so reluctant to consider God's existence that he said a more likely explanation for life on earth would be that "at some earlier time, somewhere in the universe, a civilization evolved . . . to a very high level of technology, and designed a form of life they seeded onto this planet."[7]

You read that right—the best-known atheist in the world thinks the plot of *Prometheus*, Ridley Scott's prequel to his classic *Alien* franchise, is more plausible than the existence of a loving, creator God.

In the secular worldview, everything exists accidentally. Nothing is of ultimate consequence. There is no explanation and no purpose behind our existence; Dr. Krauss himself has often referred to "the illusion of purpose."[8]

What does it say about Christianity that some of the greatest, most captivating modern stories like *Star Wars*, *Lord of the Rings*, *The Matrix*, *Harry Potter*, *Superman*, and many others borrow so heavily from Christianity, while no one is writing songs, books, or screenplays about the world Krauss and Dawkins describe—the world that shouldn't really exist, full of people who don't really matter? Because there's nothing compelling about that story. Because that story is not true.

John Polkinghorne was a physics and mathematics professor at Cambridge and the president of Queens College. He wrote, "For me, the fundamental content for belief in God is that there is a Mind and a Purpose behind the history of the universe, and that the One whose veiled presence is intimated in this way is worthy of worship and the ground of hope."[9]

Becoming a Christian isn't just about a religious experience. Some people become Christians because belief in a loving God is more rational than atheism, and because Jesus is the clearest, most evident revelation of God the world has ever seen. Even if you're highly educated, even if you're doubtful, open your mind to the possibility of faith in Christ today.

Today's Scripture

"Before the mountains were brought forth, or ever You had formed the earth and the world, Even from everlasting to everlasting, You *are* God." (Psalm 90:2 NKJV)

"This I say, therefore, and testify in the Lord, that you should no longer walk as the rest of the Gentiles walk, in the futility of their mind, having their understanding darkened, being alienated from the life of God, because of the ignorance that is in them, due to the blindness of their heart." (Ephesians 4:17-18 NKJV)

Today's Prayer

Help me quiet my mind for a moment today, and to pray a simple prayer. Like a child who needs his or her father, I need You. I love You with all my mind, this mind that You created. Thank You.

DAY 24

CAN GOD AND EVOLUTION COEXIST?

Summer 1996. Church camp. I went hoping to play basketball and maybe fall in love with a girl at the Thursday night dance. Yes, Methodist church camps have dances. On Wednesday night I sat in an outdoor amphitheater, sweaty and pimple-faced (my chances for romance dwindling), listening to the featured speaker. I don't remember anything he said about Jesus—just what he said about science and evolution.

"You can believe God, or you can believe scientists, but you can't believe both," he said. "Evolution is a lie, and those who believe it are lost."

I was skeptical, to say the least. I liked my science teacher. Mr. Harbison was smart and kind, and he cared about his students. He wasn't demonic; he was Presbyterian.

During my time in college, I found that all the brightest professors and students were avid evolutionists. I did my own reading on evolutionary biology and concluded that Darwin's theory probably offers a more thorough explanation of how we got here than anything else I'd read—including the Bible. I decided religion is just an outdated, well-intentioned attempt to explain our existence and to express the awe and gratitude people naturally feel when we consider the universe and our unlikely place in it.

Like many atheists, I came to believe "It's an astonishing stroke of luck that we are here. The universe could so easily have remained lifeless and simple—just physics and chemistry, just the scattered dust of the cosmic explosion that gave birth to time and space. The fact that life evolved out of literally nothing, 10 billion years after the universe evolved out of nothing . . . and not only did evolution happen: it eventually led to beings capable of comprehending the process by which they comprehend it."[10]

For several years, this seemed to me a better explanation than "God made everything in six days," and at the time, it appeared to render the Bible obsolete.

These days, I wince every time I think back to that message I heard at church camp. I hate it when Christians say stupid things (myself included). I'm sorry that guys who say things like "You can believe in God or science, but not both" were given a microphone and a paycheck to speak to impressionable young minds at a Christian event. I'm sorry we've made it seem like God and science are at war. I'm sorry I didn't fall in love at church camp (but to be honest, it wasn't really *love* I was hoping for, if you know what I mean).

Is evolution an affront to theology, or can the two coexist? It depends on what we mean by *evolution*. For some, Darwin's theory provides the simplest and best explanation for how life on earth has developed over time. But for many avid secularists, Darwin's theory was the last nail in religion's coffin. Respected philosopher Dan Dennett, for example, has branded evolution the "'universal acid' for any tendency toward religious thinking."[11] So which is it? Is evolution a helpful theory that neither threatens nor bolsters theological conviction? Or did Darwin kill God once and for all?

Over a century ago, Chesterton addressed these very questions. "Evolution," he wrote,

> is either an innocent scientific description of how certain earthly things came about; or, if it is anything more than this, it is an attack upon thought itself. If evolution destroys anything, it does not destroy religion but rationalism. If evolution simply means that a positive

thing called an ape turned very slowly into a positive thing called a man, then it is stingless for the most orthodox; for a personal God might just as well do things slowly as quickly, especially if, like the Christian God, he were outside time.[12]

I think there's been a misunderstanding. What if evolution was never meant to pose a threat to creation? Evolution is agnostic; it is unconcerned about the supernatural questions of life's origins or purpose. Evolutionists believe simpler life forms become more complex over time through processes of natural selection, and those processes need not pose a threat to your belief in a Creator who set those processes into motion.

As a creationist, I believe God is responsible for the existence of the universe and everything in it. To be clear, I'm not one of those "Young Earth Creationists" who believe this world is four thousand to six thousand years old because that's how all the numbers add up in the Bible. I don't claim to know exactly how God made everything, or how long it took, or how He continues to create new things all the time. More important, I don't think that what a person believes about evolution is essential to their salvation in Christ. It's just as easy to be an evolutionist and a faithful Christian as it is to be a creationist and a spiteful jerk.

Scott Jones, a United Methodist bishop, and his son, Arthur, a United Methodist pastor, frame the creation-evolution conversation this way:

What if the fight over the last two hundred years is pointless, and we discover that there are amazing commonalities between the findings of science and the story of life found in Scripture? Genesis describes the creation in a step-by-step process; science tells us that all living things evolved.... Genesis tells us to take care of the earth because it is a gift, and Jesus made it clear that everyone on earth is our neighbor;

science posits that we are all connected. Maybe, finally, that is where we will find unity between science and religion: the miracle of life.[13]

We've been deceived by extremists—within religious and academic circles alike—to believe that faith and science are natural enemies. They're *not*. Half of all professional scientists in America believe in some kind of Higher Power, which led Harvard evolutionist Stephen Jay Gould to write, "Either half my colleagues are enormously stupid, or else the science of Darwinism is fully compatible with conventional religious beliefs—and equally compatible with atheism."[14]

What if "faith versus science" is a false choice? What if God loves science?

Today's Scripture

"Great are the works of the LORD; they are pondered by all who delight in them." (Psalm 111:2)

Today's Prayer

Today I pray that Your church would become a community where people learn not just what to think, but how to think. If there is some way I can help make this happen, I pray for the courage to be assertive.

DAY 25

Even if I Believed in God, How Could I Possibly Explain Myself?

Let's talk about Noah and the ark, the story that's depicted on the cover of every children's Bible, with the cute little giraffe poking his head out the window like he's Dino from *The Flintstones*. My first question is, WHY IS THAT STORY FEATURED IN A CHILDREN'S BIBLE?! It's *absolutely horrifying*. When I read to my kids about all the death and devastation of a flood that covered the whole earth, they always have similar questions:

> *Daddy, did* all *the other animals die?* Yes, baby.
> *Daddy, did all the other red pandas die?* Yes, sweetie.
> *Daddy, did all the other puppies drownd-ed too?* [At this point, I'm too sad to respond!]

Atheists and agnostics will often point to Noah's ark as a prime example of why they could never believe in the God of the Bible. They wonder how any educated person can believe in stories like Noah's ark. Every kind of animal, together on one boat? Did those two lions happen to be vegetarians? Where did Noah find two polar bears in tropical Mesopotamia?

Explaining stories like Noah's ark to my educated, non-Christian friends presents a real challenge. They expect me to say that I think it's fiction or "just a myth." But I believe Noah's ark is based on actual

93

events. We know there really was a devastating, regional flood around 5600 BC.[15] That's why every major civilization in Mesopotamia had a flood story explaining the catastrophe from their perspective, and usually in theological terms. In other words, they explained why their gods punished humankind with that awful flood of which their ancestors spoke.

But I also believe Noah wasn't the first story written about that flood. The Sumerians, Assyrians, and Babylonians all told stories in which their gods sent the flood after telling a guy to build a boat and save some animals. Those civilizations were hundreds of years older than the Hebrew culture that produced the story of Noah, and it seems likely that this story was an adaptation of those older flood narratives.

If that's so, would it mean the Bible isn't true? No—it means something far more interesting. It means the ancient Hebrews, who *knew* those other stories, wanted to tell a different story *for a reason*. They wanted to tell the world how their God was different.

In those older stories, the gods sent the floods for the most arbitrary reasons. In one story, people are too loud and it gives the gods a headache. In another, the gods are just annoyed with people. In some flood stories, there's no reason given at all. It's just arbitrary death and destruction at the hands of the impervious gods. As the people and animals drowned to death, those gods laughed. They kept their distance. Some even cowered in fear—afraid of the very storm they created.

Enter Noah. In the Hebrew story, God sends the Flood because His heart is broken by all the senseless, irredeemable violence that covers the earth. Wars. Tribal conflicts. Physical and sexual abuse of women and children. There was so much violence, with so many innocent people living in fear, that God wanted to start over to give people another chance to love and know Him.

In the story, God speaks to Noah—the only righteous man on earth—and hatches a plan to save humanity. The rains fall, the waters rise, and then it is finished. Noah and his family find dry land and begin to start over. They are traumatized, but they are not alone. The one true God meets them there. He blesses them, commands them to repopulate the earth, and proposes to them, like a man in love proposes to his future bride. God says,

> "I now establish my covenant with you and with your descendants after you and with every living creature that was with you....Never again will all life be destroyed by the waters of a flood; never again will there be a flood to destroy the earth." And God said, "This is the sign of the covenant I am making between me and you and every living creature with you, a covenant for all generations to come: I have set my rainbow in the clouds, and it will be the sign of the covenant between me and the earth." (Genesis 9:8-13)

This is not a god who laughs or cowers or keeps his distance while people suffer. This is the one true God who comes and meets us on our turf to show us we're never alone. He proposes a covenant with us—which was something no ancient god had ever done before. The Hebrew people wrote about Noah to tell the world about an altogether different kind of God.

There are brilliant, intellectual Christians whom I respect and trust and who believe Noah's ark is a literal, historical account. I'm not saying they're wrong. I'm saying you don't have to agree with them in order to believe the Bible is true and to make Jesus the center of your life.

And the lions weren't vegetarians.

They ate the unicorns.

Today's Scripture

"Have I not commanded you? Be strong and of good courage; do not be afraid, nor be dismayed, for the LORD your God *is* with you wherever you go." (Joshua 1:9 NKJV)

"I am with you always, to the very end of the age."

(Jesus in Matthew 28:20)

Today's Prayer

I have always cared too much about what other people will think. Help me to seek the Truth, regardless of others' opinions. And grant me the courage to tell my friends a different story about a different kind of God.

WEEK 6

DOUBTS ABOUT QUALITY OF LIFE

An atheist believes that a hospital should be built instead of a church. An atheist believes that deed must be done instead of prayer said. An atheist strives for involvement in life and not escape into death. He wants disease conquered, poverty vanished, war eliminated.

—Madalyn Murray O'Hair

"Then the King will say to those on his right, 'Come, you who are blessed by my Father; take your inheritance, the kingdom prepared for you since the creation of the world. For I was hungry and you gave me something to eat, I was thirsty and you gave me something to drink, I was a stranger and you invited me in, I needed clothes and you clothed me, I was sick and you looked after me, I was in prison and you came to visit me.'

"Then the righteous will answer him, 'Lord, when did we see you hungry and feed you, or thirsty and give you something to drink? When did we see you a stranger and invite you in, or needing clothes and clothe you? When did we see you sick or in prison and go to visit you?'

"The King will reply, 'Truly I tell you, whatever you did for one of the least of these brothers and sisters of mine, you did for me.'"

—*Jesus of Nazareth*
(Matthew 25:34-40)

DAY 26

Why Doesn't Belief in God Make Your Life Easier?

It seems like becoming a believer should come with some benefits, and I don't mean a swanky mansion in the afterlife either. I want some real-life bennies. If God is real and good, then giving your life to Him should make things easier, more convenient, less painful. But that's not what happens, is it? Giving your life to Christ doesn't change your circumstances, does it? People who get baptized in the middle of a crisis are often disappointed when they find out the holy water didn't put their fires out.

Becoming a Christian doesn't come with a pain-free guarantee. Some of my closest friends are faithful believers who can't get pregnant and don't know why. Another friend is a pastor who is taking care of his mother as she stumbles into early-onset Alzheimer's; she's only fifty-eight, but she doesn't know her own kids' names. It sucks, and it feels unfair.

But the more I think about it, I'm not sure where my idea of fair even comes from. The assumption that life should be fair and bad things shouldn't happen to "good people" is a very modern concept. The Bible never promises believers they won't suffer, and the first Christians certainly didn't expect a pain-free life.

As an example, take the apostle Paul, the second-most important figure in Christian history. He had a good life as a Pharisee, a well-to-do religious professional. He was respected and upwardly mobile. Around AD 35, just a few years after Jesus's death and resurrection, Paul was put in charge of the anti-Christian initiative, and he was responsible for terrorizing the first believers. He and his henchmen dragged people out of their own homes and humiliated them in the streets. Paul presided over the execution of the first Christian martyr, Stephen.

But then Jesus appeared to Paul, and everything changed. He became a Christian—giving up his upward mobility, reputation, and status—and soon after, he started planting churches. You'd think God would reward His faithfulness by blessing Paul with comfort and wealth, but the more he did for God, the harder his life became. In 2 Corinthians 11, Paul listed everything he survived, and it's painful to read: he was beaten, stoned, arrested, shipwrecked, robbed, naked, cold, hungry, and shipwrecked *again* (see 2 Corinthians 11:23-27).

Considering all Paul went through, you'd think God would at least let the man be ruggedly handsome, right? Wrong. According to the only accounts we have that refer to Paul's appearance, he wasn't exactly a Hemsworth. He was puny and weak (see 2 Corinthians 10:10), blind as a bat (see Galatians 6:11), and single into middle age (see 1 Corinthians 7:8). Someone who claimed to know Paul called him "a man of middling size, and his hair was scanty, and his legs were a little crooked, and his knees were far apart; he had large eyes, and his eyebrows met, and his nose was somewhat long."[1]

Can you imagine Paul, after giving his life to Jesus and planting twenty or more churches and suffering persecution and imprisonment, looking in the mirror one morning and thinking, "Seriously, God? A unibrow?"

Paul's weightiest problems were spiritual. The most influential Christian in history struggled with sin: "I do not understand what I do. For what I want to do I do not do, but what I hate I do" (Romans 7:15). God didn't even protect Paul from temptation.

So how did Paul explain his suffering? Did he say it's unfair? Why didn't he just quit the moment Jesus failed to make his life better? Paul explains it in Romans 8:28: "And we know that in all things God works for the good of those who love him, who have been called according to his purpose."

During the Holocaust, only one in twenty-eight prisoners survived the Nazi concentration camps. An Austrian Jew named Viktor Frankl survived imprisonment in four different camps, where he witnessed some of the worst atrocities ever committed by men. Although he went through hell on earth alongside millions of other desperate men, women, and children, Frankl refused to allow the immense pain to crush his spirit.

On one occasion, Frankl wrote:

> It seemed to me that I would die in the near future. In this critical situation, however, my concern was different from that of most of my comrades. Their question was, "Will we survive the camp? For, if not, all this suffering has no meaning." The question which beset me was, "Has all this suffering, this dying around us, a meaning? For, if not, then ultimately there is no meaning to survival; for a life whose meaning depends upon such a happenstance—as whether one escapes or not—ultimately would not be worth living at all."[2]

Just because bad things happen to you doesn't mean God is doing those things to punish you. Sometimes bad things happen because the world is broken; other times bad things happen because the Enemy is a beast. Sometimes bad things happen because people are idiots; other times bad things happen because you're an idiot. And sometimes bad things happen for no good reason at all.

Jesus won't keep you from pain; in fact, sometimes following Jesus will lead you to feel *more* pain. But the difference Jesus makes is this: He *always* works in your pain to redeem it, to make something beautiful out of your mess.

Jesus never promised to make your life easier. He promises to make your life matter.

Today's Scripture

"I consider that our present sufferings are not worth comparing with the glory that will be revealed in us." (Romans 8:18)

Today's Prayer

I am no longer my own, but Yours. Put me to what You will, rank me with whom You will; put me to doing, put me to suffering; let me be employed for You, or laid aside for You, exalted for You, or brought low for You; let me be full, let me be empty, let me have all things, let me have nothing. I freely and wholeheartedly yield all things to Your pleasure and disposal. And now, glorious and blessed God, Father, Son, and Holy Spirit, You are mine and I am yours. So be it. And the covenant now made on earth, let it be ratified in heaven. Amen.[3]

DAY 27

WHY AREN'T CHRISTIANS ANY *HAPPIER*?

A common assumption is that finding God should make you happy. I mean, He's invisible after all, so finding Him is quite an accomplishment. And being able to talk to God on a regular basis, and knowing that He cares about you so much that He would even suffer and die for you—that's a pretty big deal. If you really believe that's true, it seems like it should be enough to put a smile on your face.

But Christians don't seem to be much happier than anybody else. In my independent, unscientific study, people with Jesus fishes and cross stickers on their cars are just as likely to get upset when I cut them off in traffic as Subaru drivers with Darwin-legged fishes and NPR stickers are. The other day, I came across a Christian lady in the grocery store whose shirt read "Too Blessed to Be Depressed." Is that how it works? Because I'm betting Christians suffer with depression at the same rate as non-Christians do.

I think one of the worst lies we've ever been told is that we're all supposed to be happy. Advertisers tell you that lie, and social media does, too. Everyone looks happy on Snapchat; I mean, they have rainbows pouring from their mouths! You only see your friends' happiest moments on Instagram.

Christianity hasn't offered much of an alternative message. It's like at some point we saw how advertisers were getting rich, and the church became just another merchant of "happiness." We wanted people to know that Pepsi might make you happy, but not as happy as God can make you. It was unintentional, but we marketed Jesus like a product, putting him on the same level as a Volkswagen. "German engineering is OK, but have you tried Jewish carpentry?"

It's not that God doesn't want you to be happy; it's just that happiness isn't your purpose. Jesus lived the most purposeful life ever, but even He wasn't always happy. Jesus promised us life will hurt and we are going to suffer. The point of following Him isn't to avoid the pain; the point is to let Jesus use your pain to redeem you and to give hope to others hurting around you.

Jesus said, "I am the true vine, and my Father is the gardener . . . every branch in me that bears no fruit, while every branch that does bear fruit he prunes so that it will be even more fruitful" (John 15:1-2). The "branch that bears fruit" is a reference to believers, so Jesus is saying that sometimes God "prunes" or "cuts" us back for the purpose of making our lives more fruitful.

The other day I heard a young preacher say that the time his faith grew the most was when he had cancer. Battling a life-threatening disease gave him a sense of perspective that escapes most of us in our day-to-day grind. When you're fighting cancer, it doesn't matter who wins *The Bachelor* or who's in the White House.

That preacher got down on the floor and played with his kids every day, even though he was exhausted and nauseated from the chemo. He got on his knees and prayed and read his Bible every day. He made more eye contact with his wife, and yeah, they cried a lot. But they also laughed more hysterically than ever. Cancer didn't make him happy, obviously, but while he had cancer, he discovered *joy*.

Joy is not the same as happiness. Happiness is reliant on your circumstances; joy springs up, regardless of your circumstances. Happiness is temporary; joy is eternal. You may find happiness at certain moments and in certain things, but you can have joy at all times and in all things by choosing to be grateful and awestruck by God every day, no matter what you're up against.

Today's Scripture

"Bring joy to your servant, Lord, for I put my trust in you." (Psalm 86:4)

"Be joyful in hope, patient in affliction, faithful in prayer."
(Romans 12:12)

Today's Prayer

I've been chasing happiness, when I should have been resting in Your grace. Today I choose joy, and I pray that the joy welling up within me will point others toward You, the source of all joy.

DAY 28

WHY ARE CHRISTIANS NO FUN?

Confession time: I love dark TV shows and movies. The bloodier the better. I like to share a bottle of wine with my wife over dinner. I happen to think sex is fun, whether or not you're making a baby. I laugh at raunchy stand-up comedy. I curse—not a lot, just when I'm alone in my car, or coaching Little League (I don't curse *at* the boys, just in my mind sometimes, like when little Timmy would rather roll in the grass than play respectable right field defense).

Like anyone, if I had to choose between heaven and hell, I'd rather go to heaven. But if heaven is full of straitlaced Christians who don't curse in traffic and who judge me for drinking, and if hell is full of comedians, rock stars, and rebels … well, I just don't know. Last year, my city was brought to its knees when Hurricane Harvey dropped fifty inches of rain on us. Eighty-two people died, and tens of thousands of people were displaced by the floods. It was a nightmare of apocalyptic proportion.

Four months later, my church gathered for our first Christmas Eve since Harvey. Because everyone was still dealing with PTSD, I decided to use my Christmas Eve sermon as an opportunity to help people relax and laugh a little. So, in the middle of our Christmas Eve candlelight service, I showed a clip of my favorite news segment during Harvey. The segment was shot from inside a rescue boat, where some middle-aged men from Louisiana (known locally as the Louisiana Cajun Navy) were tending to a family they had just rescued from the flood.

When the oldest Cajun in the boat took a bottle of what was obviously vodka, poured it into a shot glass, and offered it to one of the victims, the female news anchor back in the studio said, "Look at that—he's giving them some water," to which the male anchor responded, "Yeah...I don't think that's water." Then, as if on cue, the old Cajun hero produced another bottle—this one had an *Ozarka* label—and the male anchor said, "Ah! There's the water!"

Then I offered my traumatized community some hope by saying, "It's OK to party at Christmas, especially after the year we've had. For Joseph and Mary, Jesus was their party after a really hard year. Joy is who Jesus is. Jesus is the party. Jesus is a shot of vodka in a rescue boat when your house is underwater."

Most people got what I was trying to say, but predictably, a few hardcore Christians were outraged that I would compare Jesus to a shot of vodka. Those emails are always fun to read on Christmas morning.

Sometimes I don't get why believers are such a buzzkill. When the church was born, the first Christians threw the craziest parties. There were men and women eating and drinking, singing and dancing, and even if they came from different places and spoke different languages, they loved God and understood one another. The first church was so party-heavy that the very first criticism levied against it by those on the outside was, "They are full of new wine" (Acts 2:13).

To be clear, "new wine" had higher alcohol content than regular wine. They could've said, "They're full of wine," but that wouldn't have done justice to what was happening in the church. Those Christians didn't just look *drunk*, they looked *sloppy* drunk.

Of course they weren't drunk...at least not on wine. God's Spirit was moving in them, flying them high as kites. They were so elated to be in God together that their church services looked like raves.

I don't know when Christians stopped having fun.

Most people look at the Bible as the problem. They see a long list of rules, followed by Jesus, followed by another long list of rules. But the Bible isn't the problem; it's less than 3 percent rules, and it's 35 percent poetry, and it's 100 percent story. It's full of humor (remember that talking donkey?), family drama, suspense, romance, and sex. Try to read these verses from the Song of Songs without blushing:

> My beloved is to me a sachet of myrrh resting between my breasts. My beloved is to me a cluster of henna blossoms from the vineyards. With great delight I sat in his shadow, and his fruit was sweet to my taste. He brought me to the banqueting house, and his intention toward me was love. I am my beloved's, and his desire is for me. Come, my beloved, let us go forth into the fields, and lodge in the villages; let us go out early to the vineyards, and see whether the vines have budded, whether the grape blossoms have opened and the pomegranates are in bloom. There I will give you my love. (1:13-14; 2:3-4; 2:16; 7:11-12)

That's so hot! So how did Christians get so ... *cold*? I think the problem is religion. Religion is all about control. And when religious leaders take hold of something powerful like the Bible, they instinctively twist it to control people. Does the Bible give people boundaries and rules to live by? Yes. But are those rules meant to manipulate and scare people into submission? No!

One time I went to hear a popular artist speak at a museum in Kansas City. She looked exactly how you'd expect a modern artist to look. Dreadlocks. Tattoos. Her skirt looked like a tablecloth from the Cracker Barrel. Full hipster. After her lecture, she took some questions from local art students. One of them asked her how and when she decides to begin painting.

And she said, "The first step in the creative process is knowing your boundaries. I'd love to paint the whole city, but I can't. Before I paint I need a canvas; I need to know its dimensions." Then it hit me: freedom isn't doing whatever you want. Freedom is knowing the size of your canvas, and being unafraid to begin.

That's what following Jesus is all about. There are rules, sure, but their only purpose is to make you more alive, more joyful, and more creative. With Jesus, no matter your past or present circumstances, you're free to live.

So don't be afraid to start living today.

Today's Scripture

"Though you have not seen him, you love him; and even though you do not see him now, you believe in him and are filled with an inexpressible and glorious joy, for you are receiving the end result of your faith, the salvation of your souls." (1 Peter 1:8-9)

"Restore to me the joy of your salvation." (Psalm 51:12)

Today's Prayer

Thank You for setting me free, even though sometimes I still live like I'm in chains. Today I want to be so full of pure joy that people who see me wonder how much I've had to drink. In Jesus's name.

DAY 29

WHY DO CHRISTIANS TREAT LIBERALS LIKE THE ENEMY?

L et's say you didn't know what a liberal was, and you spent a few days talking to evangelicals at a Christian conference. I'm afraid you'd come away from that experience believing liberals are the ghastly products of an unholy union between Marxist socialism and militant atheism. In many circles (including twenty-four-hour news networks), "liberal" has become synonymous with "secular," and "Christian" with "conservative." Some churches, outspoken Christian leaders, and conservative media personalities have made it clear that the line between Christianity and liberal politics should not (and *cannot*) be crossed.

But what about Jesus? Feed-the-poor, take-care-of-prisoners, blessed-are-the-peacemakers Jesus. I could be wrong, and I have no evidence to back this up, but that guy seems like a hippie to me. Last I checked, there weren't many hippies hanging out at the Republican National Convention. If Jesus was a liberal, why are so many Christians conservative? And why do so many of my liberal friends feel so judged by the Christians in their lives?

The truth of the matter is that extreme conservatives and extreme liberals can be equally manipulative and equally damaging to the fabric of our culture. Essentially, they're the same people; they just get mad about different things. They're invariably blind about their own hypocrisy. They are the conservatives who will condemn you for being gay and then, with no questions asked, welcome someone who's been divorced several times (even though Jesus said nothing about homosexuality and clearly condemned divorce). They are the liberals who get up in arms about poverty and aren't moved at all by the sixty million unborn babies aborted in America since 1973.

I can explain why most conservative people in the world are religious; people who lean conservative tend to come from religious families. I can't explain why so many Christians treat liberals like the enemy, although I will say, having lived in both the evangelical and liberal worlds at different points in my life, political marginalization is a two-way street. Some on the left can be just as bitter and hateful toward conservatives as some on the right have been toward liberals.

Furthermore, it's debatable whether Jesus can be defined as liberal by today's standards. He had a lot to say about hell, sin, judgment, sexual ethics, absolute Truth, and personal holiness—stuff that tends to make many social progressives squirm.

Jesus was equally welcoming—and equally critical—of those with conservative and liberal worldviews. To those on the right who used their Bibles to judge and condemn, Jesus said, "You hypocrites! You shut the door of the kingdom of heaven in people's faces. You yourselves do not enter, nor will you let those enter who are trying to!" (Matthew 23:13). To those on the left who were living as if morality and truth are relative, Jesus said things like, "Go and sin no more," and "Girl, you've been married five times, and now you're shacking up with bae?!" (John 4:18, paraphrase).

Throughout the Bible, it's tough to pin down God's politics. Sometimes God is all about building walls (see Nehemiah 2:17) and other times, he wants walls to come down (see Joshua 6:20). In the New Testament, the first Christians are happy to feed the poor and hungry (hippies!), but they also believed "the one who is unwilling to work shall not eat" because no-strings-attached charity can cause idleness and laziness (2 Thessalonians 3:6-10, especially v. 10).

It seems to me that God is too big to fit into any political party and, no matter your affiliation, Jesus will always challenge you to love beyond what you once thought possible. God calls Christians to think with conservative minds, by living frugally and using common sense, and to love with liberal hearts, by looking out for those who are lost, lonely, or vulnerable. Most important, it seems to me there's room enough on Jesus's bandwagon for people from all walks of life—so long as our faith in Jesus drives our politics, and not the other way around.

Today's Scripture

"Behold, how good and how pleasant *it is* For brethren to dwell together in unity!" (Psalm 133:1)

"I exhort first of all that supplications, prayers, intercessions, and giving of thanks be made for all men, for kings and all who are in high authority, that we may lead a quiet and peaceable life in all godliness and reverence." (1 Timothy 2:1-2 NKJV)

Today's Prayer

Forgive me for judging people who think, live, and vote differently than I do. Help me to go out of my way to understand, respect, and love people the way that You do. And strengthen me to live, think, and speak in ways that lead people to You today. Thank You.

DAY 30

MOST CHRISTIANS ARE HYPOCRITES; WHY WOULD I WANT TO BE ONE?

There's a group of hipsters who work at a salon near my house. They each have more tattoos than the Duggars have kids. They color their hair gray *on purpose*. When I told them I'm a Methodist they said, "Is that like a Mormon?" I cringed. But every time I go in for a haircut, they smile, they know my name, and they offer me free beer. My stylist, Ronaldo, greets me with a special handshake that I always manage to screw up, and he tells me he likes my shoes.

For the next forty-five minutes, Rolando tells me all about his softball team, his ailing *abuela*, his growing business, and his boyfriend. We talk about *Star Wars* and Bruno Mars. Once, he opened up to me about the time his father was murdered. Once, he asked me to pray for him. He *always* asks me about my church, and he always promises to come check out a service soon.

The whole experience is so great that I almost look forward to getting a haircut. *Almost.* I enjoy spending time with those agnostic hipsters every bit as much as I like hanging out with hardcore Christians. Sometimes hanging out with Christians can feel like the Righteousness Olympics…like we're all competing to project an image of morality and self-sufficiency. Which is hard to do because we're all such a mess on the inside.

When I mentioned to a few pastors that I go to a salon where no one is Christian and my stylist is gay, one of them said, "You're compromising the gospel by going there, brother. Drop the Word on them, and get out of there."

Why would I want to be like that guy? Ronaldo may be a sinner, but at least he's not a hypocrite.

According to a recent study, between 80 to 90 percent of nonreligious Americans believe Christians are "somewhat hypocritical" or "very hypocritical."[4] Jesus used the word *hypocrite* to poke fun at the superreligious Pharisees. *Hypocrite* is a Greek word that literally means "stage actor." By calling religious guys "hypocrites," he was saying they're "acting" holy on the surface even though they're rotten on the inside.

We all know Christians who talk one way and walk another. But hypocrisy doesn't begin with bad behavior; it starts with false expectations. Like everybody else, Christians are bound to sin. Jesus's little brother James wrote, "If anyone, then, knows the good they ought to do and doesn't do it, it is sin for them" (James 4:17); I've done that three times already since I sat down to write today's devotion.

What makes us hypocrites is when we judge other people (like Ronaldo) because their sin is somehow worse than ours. Jesus said, "Do not judge, or you too will be judged.... Why do you look at the speck of sawdust in your brother's eye and pay no attention to the plank in your own eye?" (Matthew 7:1-3).

When you're a Christian, you're not trying to be like other Christians. You're trying to be like Jesus. You can have a beer with agnostics and be a Christian. You can get a haircut from an openly gay man and be a Christian. You can make fun of twenty-something hipsters with gray hair and be a Christian. But you can't alienate God's children with your arrogant hypocrisy and be a Christian.

Jesus said, "You are the light of the world.... Let your light shine before men, that they may see your good works and glorify your Father in heaven" (Matthew 5:14, 16).

Wherever you go today, and whoever you're with, let the light of

Christ shine through you, so that some who might be far from God, and some who might be jaded by Christian hypocrisy, will know that God is love and Jesus is Lord.

Today's Scripture

"If someone says, 'I love God,' and hates his brother, he is a liar; for he who does not love his brother whom he has seen, how can he love God whom he has not seen?" (1 John 4:20)

Today's Prayer

I want to shine Your light today, God. I want people to know that following Jesus is about joy, not judgment, and hope, not hypocrisy. Help me to be Your messenger today.

DOUBTS ABOUT SEX AND RELATIONSHIPS

Everything in the world is about sex except sex. Sex is about power.

—*Oscar Wilde*

DAY 31

WHY WOULD GOD CARE WHO I SLEEP WITH?

One thing that's always bothered me about Christians is how judgy we can be about sex. Growing up in church, I got the distinct impression that sex is dangerous and scary, sexual sin is the worst kind of sin, and a single woman is somehow more valuable to guys when she's a virgin.

Male virginity, on the other hand, was seen as sweet, but sad. Don't ask me how I know that.

One time when I was in the eighth grade, my friend Colin gave me a VHS (kids, ask your parents) copy of the movie *Basic Instinct*, which made headlines for its steamy sexual content. I was really more interested in the artful screenwriting—nah, I'm lying; I wanted to see Sharon Stone naked. Anyway, I got busted, and when my youth pastor found out, he told me how disappointed he was in me for watching what amounted to porn.

It was wrong of me, no doubt about it. I wasn't ready for the things I saw in that movie. But if I'm honest, the most disturbing images I saw weren't sexual in nature; the murdered corpse lying on the bed, the terrifying lead character, the horrific violence, and Sharon Stone's acting were all far more insidious. But in that youth pastor's mind, the only part of that movie that I shouldn't have seen was the sex.

Why do Christians care so much about people's sex lives? Why can't we just focus on helping others, you know? Doesn't God care more about poverty and violence than who people choose to sleep with?

You wouldn't know it by reading about Christianity's history with sex. In the fourth century, church leaders decided Mary (Jesus's mom) was not only a virgin when she conceived Jesus, but she never had sex with any man—not even Joseph. They thought sex was dirty, you see, and Mary had to be pure. So they declared her a perpetual virgin, and church leaders even went so far as to manufacture the false narrative that Joseph must have been a widower who conceived Jesus's half-siblings (who are mentioned in the New Testament) with his deceased first wife. According to this fiction, Joseph took in the much younger Mary and cared for her as a father might, without ever pursuing a sexual relationship with her. Mind you, none of this is even remotely supported by the New Testament, which just goes to show you the lengths to which some religious people will go to keep human sexuality under control.

Sadly, Christianity's vise grip on sexual expression didn't end with Mary and Joseph. In the fifth century, Bishop Augustine declared that having sex for pleasure—even within marriage—was a sin. Following suit, Bishop Jerome delivered this zinger in a sermon: "Any man who is too passionate a lover—even with his own wife—is an adulterer."[1] I wonder how many husbands, on their way home from church that day, told their wives, "See, honey? I wasn't tired; I was following the bishop's orders."

At one point in time, the church restricted sex on Thursdays (because Jesus was arrested on a Thursday), on Fridays (because Jesus was killed on a Friday), on Saturdays (because Jesus was dead on a Saturday), and on Sundays (because Jesus rose from the grave on a Sunday). Add in the forty-day fasts before major holidays, as well as other special occasions, and you'll see how for many years, married Christians were only allowed to have sex forty-four days a year!

So yes, the church has overreached at times. Yes, Christian leaders have typically been terrified of sex. I used to resent that about Christianity; I used to think it was about controlling people. Over time, I've come to see it differently; I've realized, at its heart, the true Christian message about sex is meant to position believers to have the most amazing sex imaginable.

What changed my opinion? Reading the Bible for myself. The Bible is more sexually liberated than people seem to think. From the wild, erotic poetry of Song of Songs to the apostle Paul's insistence that a married couple should pretty much be having sex all the time (see 1 Corinthians 7:1-5), the Bible is unabashedly sex-positive.

Christians don't set limits around sexual expression because sex is so bad; we need boundaries because sex is so good. We need boundaries around sex like we need the suggested serving size on a package of bacon; without healthy parameters, we'll ruin the gift and destroy ourselves in the process. God doesn't judge sexual sin more harshly than any other sins; he wants us to have the best sex on earth. But God knows the immense damage sexual sin can cause.

The best sex on earth happens when two people share an eternal covenant, based on promises they made at an altar, in front of God and their families, to love, honor, and cherish each other *no matter what*. In that context of grace and trust is where humans have *otherworldly* sex. Any sexual expression short of that is dangerous, because it puts us at risk of missing the head-spinning joy of one of God's greatest gifts.

If you've had sex outside the marriage covenant, or if you've experienced some kind of sexual trauma, on behalf of the whole church, I am sorry for the way Christians have judged and shamed you. I invite you to do what I did and read the Bible for yourself. On those pages you'll find a God who loves you and who stands ready to redeem you, because you are precious in His sight.

Today's Scripture

Let him kiss me with the kisses of his mouth—
for your love is better than wine....
My beloved is mine and I am his....

How beautiful you are, my darling!
>   Oh, how beautiful!
>   Your eyes behind your veil are doves.
Your hair is like a flock of goats....
Your teeth are like a flock of sheep just shorn,
>   coming up from the washing....
Your neck is like the tower of David,
>   built with courses of stone....
Your breasts are like two fawns,
>   like twin fawns of a gazelle
>   that browse among the lilies....
You have stolen my heart, my bride,
>   you have stolen my heart
with one glance of your eyes....
How delightful is your love, my bride!
>   How much more pleasing is your love
>   than wine!...
Eat, friends, and drink;
>   drink your fill of love.
(Song of Songs 1:2; 2:16; 4:1-2, 4-5, 9-10; 5:1)

"So they are no longer two, but one flesh. Therefore what God has joined together, let no one separate." (Jesus in Matthew 19:6)

Today's Prayer

Lord, I want to see people with Your eyes,
love people with Your heart
and serve people with Your hands today.
I'm going to need Your help.
Thank You in advance.

DAY 32

LGGBDTTTIQQAAPP?

My millennial readers may not believe me, but not long ago, there was a time when talking with friends and colleagues about human sexuality didn't result in World War III. Sex used to be a fun topic to discuss with others, but not anymore. These days, most people are simply sick of arguing and losing friends over minor differences of opinion. There are a few obvious reasons for our collective case of sex fatigue; I'll list a few here.

The Pigs Feet Test. I once went out for some Vietnamese food with a friend who happens to be Vietnamese. Over piping-hot bowls of pho, I mentioned how there seems to be a pho place on every corner in Houston. He said, "Most of them aren't legit, though."

"Pho real?!" I said (because I'm a big white dork). "How can you tell the difference between the real thing and the frauds?" He looked at me intensely and said, "If a Vietnamese restaurant doesn't have pigs feet on the menu, get up and walk out."

In Christian circles, LGBTQ inclusion is kind of like our pigs feet: we act like you can tell *everything* about a person based on this single issue. You can be a pro-America, pro-life, Southern Baptist Republican, and many conservative evangelicals still won't consider you a real Christian until you openly exclude LGBTQ people and condemn their "lifestyle."

On the other hand, you can be a social justice warrior, a friend to the poor, and a Planned Parenthood–supporting, rainbow flag–waving Bernie voter, and many liberal Christians won't accept you if you don't fully support LGBTQ marriage and ordination of LGBTQ clergy.

Call me crazy, but I don't think a person's opinions about sexual orientation should be the litmus test by which we judge the authenticity of his or her faith. Christian author Debra Hirsch made a similar point in her book *Redeeming Sex*: "Just because a heterosexual orientation might appear to be closer to God's original intent, it's by no means flawless. In fact, if we were equally honest we can probably say that most male heterosexuals are actually polyamorous in orientation; in other words, their 'natural' preference is for many sexual partners, not just one, which is clearly not what God would have originally intended. *Every human being on the planet is sexually broken. Everybody's orientation is disoriented.*"[2]

Life, Liberty, and the Pursuit of Orgasm. I'm not sure when or how it happened, but we've arrived at a curious point in human history: sex on one's own terms has become a basic human right. A person's sexual identity and expression are now every bit as sacred and protected as his or her age, race, gender, and ethnicity.

As the conversation has evolved in our culture, "LGBT" has become "LGGBDTTTIQQAAPP"—lesbian, gay, genderqueer, bisexual, demisexual, transgender, transsexual, twospirit, intersex, queer, questioning, asexual, allies, pansexual, and polyamorous—and there is no reason to think this list will ever stop growing as we continue to pride ourselves on the no-questions-asked inclusion of any and all sexual selfhoods and mores.

You Are What You Sex. I understand that sex is an important part of being human, but what does it say when a culture is literally running out of letters in its alphabet to promote and protect every possible sexual proclivity? What does it say about us that we define ourselves based on what kind of sex we're having, and with whom?

Maybe we've just got too much time on our hands. Or maybe fifty-plus years of hypersexual advertising, the glorification of eroticism in popular culture, free, unlimited pornography, and the constant objectification of women (and sometimes men) have finally brought us to our knees at the altar of Eros, the ancient god of sexual desire.

Once again, Hirsch's wisdom is essential here. During an interview on the *Maybe God* podcast, she shared a story about a gay man who came to her office seeking counseling for sex addiction. He paid to have sex with a different prostitute almost every day, but one day, something changed:

> He told me that he went into this place and a man came in and offered him his hand, and he took this man's hand, thinking it was going to lead to a sexual encounter. But the man took his hand, and he just held it. He squeezed his hand and he looked straight into his eyes, and my client said to me, "His gaze, it was just like he was peering into me.... I could see love in his eyes.... It probably only lasted for a few moments, but it felt endless. Then [he] just dropped my hand, turned around and walked out, and I began to tremble."
>
> And then he said, "I knew at that moment it wasn't sex that I wanted. I just needed a man to hold me." And he then said to me, which, I'll never forget it, "You know, I wondered whether that man ... was an angel, Debbie."[3]

Maybe sex isn't really what any of us want. Maybe what we want is love. Maybe we really want God. Nevertheless, it's a truism that we become like that which we worship, and it's possible we've worshipped sex for so long that we've come to see sexual appetite and identity—which used to be a small part of who we are—as our very essence.

There is more to say on this topic, so we'll continue the conversation tomorrow. For today, I ask you to consider these questions:

Is sex fundamentally good or bad? Why?

Do I believe sex is merely a Darwinian vehicle for the survival of our species?

Or do I believe there is something transcendent and extraordinary about the human sexual experience?

Today's Scripture

"I beseech you therefore, brethren, by the mercies of God, that you present your bodies a living sacrifice, holy, acceptable to God, which is your reasonable service." (Romans 12:1 NKJV)

Today's Prayer

Help me to worship only You today, God.

DAY 33

WHAT SEX IS BAD SEX?

According to a recent, massive study on public perceptions of Christianity, a whopping 91 percent of nonreligious young Americans (16–29) describe Christians as anti-homosexual. Eighty percent of young Christians said the same.[4] The message young adults are getting couldn't be clearer: while secular culture progresses daily toward greater sex-positivity, the church digs in its heels and refuses to budge on its archaic, puritanical doctrines.

Reading those statistics feels like a kick in the gut. I love Jesus, and I try to love everybody (Yankees fans make it hard sometimes). In my mind, God and the Bible are pro-pleasure and pro-sex. Lest we so lazily and blindly accept the opinions about sex-shaming Christians as gospel truth, here are a few things to keep in mind.

We're All Bigots. To be "sex-positive" in 2018 is to affirm all sexual orientations and behaviors equally, and to question a person's identity or expression is bigotry akin to white supremacy. Evangelical Christians are often singled out for being judgmental, but in truth, while we may have different standards, we're *all* a little judgy.

We all draw the "acceptable sex" line somewhere. For most evangelicals, it's "one man, one woman in marriage," and everything outside of that—from pornography to pedophilia—is defined as *sin*. Others draw their lines, too. For some people, it's OK for married men to watch porn, but not to sleep with other women. For others, sleeping around is OK, as long as you're in a mutually open relationship. Many think gay sex is OK, but only in monogamy. Still others think any and all sex between consenting adults is fine, but things like humiliation, violence, and pedophilia are just *wrong*.

But where do our notions of right and wrong come from? For evangelicals, it's the Bible—and that's been the source of intense scrutiny. But what about everyone else? On what foundations do liberal Christians and secularists base their beliefs about sex? What is the authoritative source of their sexual morality? Is it government? Laws? Social utility? Or, worst of all, our feelings? Why aren't these sources of morality scrutinized as acutely as the Bible has been?

We all draw our lines; for each of us, there's such a thing as bad sex. The question shouldn't be, Why are Christians so judgmental? It should be, Where, and based on what authority, do you draw the line?

Idealistic God, Realistic Savior. A running theme throughout the Bible is that God is holy, and His mission is to make us holy, too. *Holy* means "a cut above," or "distinct from the ordinary." Christians believe God created humans to be a cut above the animal kingdom and He calls believers to no longer be governed by our base impulses and desires. True human nature isn't brokenness or sin; it's holiness.

But holiness doesn't fully describe God's character; Jesus gave us a more complete image of who God is. In the Gospels, Jesus is holy, but He also has a heart. He is perfect, but He also surrounds Himself with notoriously imperfect people. John puts it this way: "The Word became flesh and dwelt among us ... full of grace and truth" (John 1:14 NKJV).

Grace *and* truth ... not just one or the other. When I think about how we draw our lines, and how sex issues are tearing us apart, it seems we've lost the ability to hold grace and truth in tension, together. Either we're all grace (live and let live, do what feels good!) or we're all truth (repent, do the right thing!) but rarely are we both.

Jesus is both. He represents the ideal Truth of God, but He came down to embrace *real* people with *real* problems in the *real* world. Yes, He surrounded Himself with sinners, but He also encouraged them not to sin anymore—and they loved Him for it! His grace inspired them to turn their lives around.

We have a lot to learn here. Christians should always be focused on the ideal kingdom of God without forsaking the pain and brokenness of the real world right in front of us. We should probably stop judging one another for being "too conservative" or "too inclusive" and simply ask God to make our hearts more like His. Because no matter where you land on LGBTQ issues, if you hope to change the world and influence people, loving them with the heart of Christ is the only place to begin.

Do I believe God's ideal for human sexual expression is one man and one woman in a loving, lifelong marriage? Yes. Does that mean anything short of that ideal is technically sinful? Yes. But should that ever stop me from loving and listening to people who don't agree with me? Of course not. Why? Because I'm a straight Christian. I've never had sex with any woman other than my wife, and I'm still the *worst* sinner I know.

To Be Honest. Protecting and honoring the dignity of all people is essential to the Christian worldview, and for far too long, LGBTQ people have been disproportionately excluded and victimized in our culture. With only a few notable exceptions, the church has done a very poor job of understanding and loving LGBTQ people. Before making any weighty comments on this subject, all Christians should be willing to take a step back and say "I'm sorry" for our complicity in the plight of God's children who happen to be LGBTQ.

I know I have been complicit at times, and I am sorry. I'm a sinner; Lord, have mercy.

Today's Scripture

"For sin shall not have dominion over you, for you are not under law but under grace." (Romans 6:14 NKJV)

Today's Prayer

God, have mercy on me, a sinner. (The tax collector's prayer from Luke 18:9-14, especially v. 13)

DAY 34

WHY ARE SINGLE PEOPLE
SINGLED OUT AT CHURCH?

Churches typically do a great job helping traditional, nuclear families learn how to become stronger families. We offer premarital counseling, marriage courses, parenting classes, children's ministries, marriage counseling, and more. But when it comes to helping single people grow, churches usually default to creating a "Singles Ministry" that amounts to something like a meat market where we hope those poor, lonely souls will eventually settle for one another.

Being a single adult can be hard, and the dating scene can be brutal, so why can't churches offer more than a sideways glance and a meat market? Does Christianity have anything better to say to single people than "Are you seeing anyone yet?"

I once served a church in rural Louisiana and a woman there was trying to start a new Sunday school class intended to bring married couples and single people together to learn about Jesus. She was really struggling to get people to come, and she came to my office to talk about it. She said, "We're doing just fine reaching married couples, but we're not having any luck with singles." So I asked her, "What's the name of the class, so I can help promote it?" And she said, "The class is called 'Pairs and Spares.'"

Pairs and Spares!

"I think I'm beginning to understand the problem," I told her. No single people in that church were going to show up to be made to feel like spare parts. And this kind of thing happens all the time in churches because too many American Christians worship the nuclear family like it's Jesus.

I'll tell you how I know that. When a thirty-five-year-old woman meets Jesus and gets baptized, her parents and maybe her best friend will show up. Her siblings might share something nice about her on Facebook. But when that same thirty-five-year-old woman meets a man and gets married, all her friends, family, coworkers, and acquaintances—basically everyone she's ever met—will show up for the wedding. And half of them will cry, because this woman *finally* met someone, which means there's hope for the rest of us.

Why do baptisms take a back seat to weddings in churches these days? Because when you worship the nuclear family, meeting a man is more important than meeting Jesus.

That's not how Christianity is supposed to work. Before we assume that people aren't complete until they're married, and that good Christians should all get married and have kids, let's remember that Jesus, the model of our faith and the subject of our worship, was a bachelor in his thirties. As was Paul, the second-most important person in the New Testament, who had this to say about marriage: "Are you free from such a commitment? Do not look for a [spouse]. But if you do marry, you have not sinned. *But those who marry will face many troubles in this life, and I want to spare you this*" (1 Corinthians 7:27-28, emphasis added).

Put *that* in a Hallmark card.

It's true that many churches have failed people who are single by giving them the impression that marriage and family are the highest human ideals. If you're single or divorced, or if you love someone who is, I hope you'll forgive Christians for getting this all wrong. And I hope you know that, according to the Bible, your most important relationships are with Jesus and the other believers with whom you share this journey of faith.

Finally, while many churches do struggle with these issues, there are congregations out there that get it. If you're struggling, find a church that fully empowers single people and dive in. I believe Jesus will meet you there.

Today's Scripture

"While Jesus was still talking to the crowd, his mother and brothers stood outside, wanting to speak to him. Someone told him, 'Your mother and brothers are standing outside, wanting to speak to you.' He replied to him, 'Who is my mother, and who are my brothers?' Pointing to his disciples, he said, 'Here are my mother and my brothers. For whoever does the will of my Father in heaven is my brother and sister and mother.' "

(Matthew 12:46-50)

Today's Prayer

Lord, I want You to be the source of my identity and my strength. Instead of searching for someone else to complete me, I choose to find my completion in You.

DAY 35

WHERE DOES GOD FIT INTO MY LOVE LIFE?

I feel like a *failure* when I'm single." —Katie, 29

I hear that line—or some version of it—from single people all the time these days, and I can understand why. On the one hand, our culture idolizes romance and sexual relationships; in all the ads, movies, and TV shows, the messaging couldn't be clearer: being in a romantic relationship is better than being alone. On the other hand, we all feel a deep, internal desire to be loved and wanted by someone. If you're single for too long, you can start to feel like the kid who gets picked last on the playground.

Why does nobody want me?

All that social pressure combined with our internal need accelerates in us the sense of urgency to find someone and be in a relationship. But whenever we put romance on such a high pedestal, we're actually hurting our chances of ever finding it. When all you can think about is not being alone anymore, whenever you become possessed with finding love (or at least a hookup), that kind of all-in obsession has a name; it's called *worship.*

I recently had a conversation with a guy who had just been through a pretty bad breakup. He really thought she was The One; for the past two years, his entire life has been consumed by their relationship. Every decision he made was based on what she wanted. He let go of childhood friends because she asked him to. She didn't like the outdoors, so he stopped camping. Literally every Instagram post he's ever made has her in it.

133

(By the way, dude, if you're reading this, it's time to go ahead and delete those. It's been several months, and it's beyond awkward.)

I felt awful for him as he told me all about their breakup. He said he didn't understand where he went wrong. He said he gave her everything he had. He said, "I worshipped the ground she walked on."

I didn't say it then because he was already crying like a baby and we were at a bar and people were staring. But here's what I was thinking: Worshipping the ground she walked on was the worst thing you ever could have done to her. It's no wonder she left you.

Why? Because worshipping the ground she walked on put her in God's place. When you do that to a person, you expect to get from them what only God is able to give you. It puts too much pressure on the person you're with; no one is strong enough to carry that kind of burden.

(You know what's really sad? If that guy really deleted all those Instagram posts with her in them, there'd be nothing left.)

But let's imagine a scenario in which she didn't break it off. Let's imagine she chose to stick with this desperate, super-clingy boyfriend of hers, and one day they got married. Eventually, she would fall apart, right? She would hurt him, turn on him, or disappoint him. Or they'd have a six-month stretch where the sex is just blah.

Even in the healthiest relationships, that's what happens.

But what if this guy has been worshipping the ground she walks on, and then one day he realizes she's not worthy of the pedestal he's put her on all these years? What if he wakes up one day and realizes she's kind of a mess, and she's always been a mess but he's been blind to it all this time, and now all he can think about is how he gave up his friends for her, how he hasn't been camping in twenty years because of her, and how he's basically wrapped his whole life around her.

It's the perfect recipe for resentment to grow in his heart, and in hers, too, because it was unfair of him to ever worship her in the first place.

When we put a romantic partner where only God belongs, we're setting the relationship up for failure. This is one reason why so many people are bitter and cynical toward the dating scene: our expectations are way too high. Even the best relationships will leave you wanting something more, and even the best sex won't satisfy your deepest longing, because we're wired to want what only God can give.

C. S. Lewis said, "If I find in myself a desire which no experience in this world can satisfy, the most probable explanation is that I was made for another world—something supernatural and eternal."[5] Instead of wondering how God fits into your love life, maybe we should all be asking, "How do romance and relationships fit into my life with God?"

Today's Scripture

"Let us therefore come boldly to the throne of grace, that we may obtain mercy and find grace to help in time of need." (Hebrews 4:16 NKJV)

Today's Prayer

God grant me the serenity
to accept the things I cannot change;
courage to change the things I can;
and the wisdom to know the difference.
Living one day at a time;
enjoying one moment at a time;
accepting hardships as the pathway to peace;
taking, as He did, this sinful world

as it is, not as I would have it;
trusting that He will make all things right
if I surrender to His Will;
that I may be reasonably happy in this life
and supremely happy with Him
forever in the next.
Amen.
(Reinhold Neibuhr, "Serenity Prayer")

DOUBTS ABOUT RELIGION

Christianity will go. It will vanish and shrink. I needn't argue with that;
I'm right and I will be proved right. We're more popular than Jesus now;
I don't know which will go first—rock and roll or Christianity.

—John Lennon

DAY 36

IF JESUS NEVER WENT TO CHURCH, WHY SHOULD I?

E ven if you believe in Jesus, why would you give your time and treasure to an institution like the church? They never seem to stop talking about money, but who really knows where all that money goes? Famous TV preachers own private Learjets and multimillion dollar homes while many of their parishioners struggle to pay their bills. Churches spend billions every year on buildings, pastors' salaries, stained glass, and fog machines, while people starve and suffer right under their noses.

Christians act as if going to church is what it means to follow Jesus, even though Jesus Himself never went to church or commanded anyone else to do so. The requirement for believers to join churches and give money seems to have been superimposed onto Christianity by the very same men who benefited from that requirement—priests, preachers, and other religious professionals.

If Jesus never went to church, then why should we?

Church attendance is not mandatory for your salvation. You can skip worship on Sundays and still go to heaven when you die. As my great-uncle used to tell his wife, "It's better to sit in a fishing boat thinking about God than it is to sit in church thinking about fishing." Going to church doesn't make you a Christian, and skipping church doesn't make you a heathen, so please don't ever feel *obligated* to worship. Going to the DMV is an obligation. Paying taxes is an obligation. Church shouldn't feel like a chore.

Jesus never intended to start an institution you feel obligated to attend; He came to give you a life you're ultimately free to live. The people who attended Jesus's sermons did so because they wanted to. And they didn't go home with a gold star for perfect attendance; they enlisted in his movement.

In fact, Jesus never even said the word *church*. No, seriously. When he's quoted saying "church" in our English translations, what he really said was *ekklesia*, a common, secular word that meant "a gathering of people called out."

Yet somehow, over hundreds of years, people started getting the idea that Jesus's *ekklesia* was a building with a steeple on top, instead of a gathering of people called out. That's when things started going south, because once *ekklesia* became *church*, people began making three lethal assumptions:

> The Church is a building...
> ...where Christians can feel safe and separate...
> ...and where priests and pastors provide for the spiritual needs of the people.

These assumptions have perpetuated the toxic myth of Christian consumerism where the church is a marketplace, people are the customers, church programs are the products, and the preacher is the salesman (who happens to work on commission).

That is *not* what Jesus had in mind. In contrast to the false assumptions we make about *ekklesia*, Jesus intended to set loose a movement of people on a mission from God. For Jesus and His followers, church was:

> 1. A revolution of grace, love, and servanthood (see Acts 2:43-47);

2. A rebel base camp, where people are trained to go to war against dark forces (see Ephesians 6:10-18)…
3. For the sake of the world (see John 3:16).

The institutions of man and the *ekklesia* of Christ are two very different things. When you get up early on a Sunday morning to go to church, I hope you have in mind Jesus and His people, not institutions or facilities. Buildings rise and fall. So do denominations and preachers and programs. But the church of Jesus Christ will endure for all time.

Today's Scripture

"And I tell you that you are Peter, and on this rock I will build my church [*ekklesia*], and the gates of Hades will not overcome it."

(Jesus, in Matthew 16:18)

"Let the word of Christ dwell in you richly in all wisdom, teaching and admonishing one another in psalms and hymns and spiritual songs, singing with grace in your hearts to the Lord." (Colossians 3:16 NKJV)

Today's Prayer

Today I pray for the church. Churches, and those in leadership, have really missed the point and caused some damage at times. But instead of just complaining, I want to be part of the solution. However You see fit today, Lord, use me to represent the true church—the revolution of grace You intended. Thank You. Amen.

DAY 37

WHY CAN'T WE JUST BE GOOD PEOPLE WHO LIVE AND LET LIVE?

It appears to me there are just as many nice, moral, good atheists as there are awful, wicked, evil Christians. Like comedian Ricky Gervais once tweeted, "I've never been insulted by hateful satanists for not believing in their devil. Only by loving Christians for not believing in their God."[1]

Some people don't seem to need God to know right from wrong or to be a decent person. Others claim to find religion so oppressive that it makes them feel *worse*, not better. If you can have a good moral compass without spending every Sunday morning and 10 percent of your income on an institution of organized religion, why be a churchgoing Christian at all?

On the other hand, it feels like a logical disconnect whenever people who don't believe in God use words like *evil*, *unfair*, or even *wrong*. Outside the realm of theology, I'm not sure these words make any sense. In strictly secular worldviews, there are no absolutes—no moral truth can be universal. Each individual person or culture gets to decide what truth is. For secular humanists in the West, the prevailing moral truth is that women should be free to dress, speak, act, and work however they wish. Paradoxically, very few Western secularists are willing to criticize the "truth" in many other parts of the world where women must cover themselves, head to toe, can't speak unless they are spoken to, and have only a fraction of the freedoms enjoyed by men. Because that's *their* truth, and although we in the West may disagree, we must be tolerant of all truths.

When secularists do try to correct false truths, their arguments

141

self-destruct. I once had a conversation with a friend at a local bar. He's agnostic, but every time we get together, we end up just talking about God. As we looked outside, we spotted two women across the street wearing hijabs, and my friend said something about how somebody should do something to free Muslim women from their oppressive culture.

> I said, "How do you know they're oppressed?"
> He said, "Because they have no choice in the matter."
> I said, "Why should they have a right to choose?"
> He said, "Because they're human beings."
> I said, "OK, but where do human rights come from?"
> He said, "In America they come from the majority vote. That's how democracy works."
> And I said, "So the majority determines our morality?" As he took a bite of his burger, I said, "What if the majority of Americans believed eating meat was immoral? Would you agree?"
> He chewed very slowly, so I continued: "Most people in the world *don't* believe women deserve equal rights; does that mean women's rights are immoral?"
> And he said, "If I buy the next round, can we change the subject?"
> I said yes.

Belief in evil—which is the ultimate Bad—requires belief in an ultimate Good. If you believe in absolute Evil (and most people do—because how else can you explain concentration camps, sex trafficking, pedophilia, and so on), you also possess an inherent sense of absolute Good. You say some Christians are evil, and I agree, but how do you come to that conclusion without some knowledge of a universal Good to which we all should aspire?

The philosopher Alvin Plantinga wrote:

Could there really be any such thing as evil if there were no God and we just evolved? I don't see how. There can be such a thing only if there is a way that rational creatures are supposed to live, obliged to live....A secular way of looking at the world has no place for genuine moral obligation of any sort...and thus no way to say there is such a thing as genuine evil. Accordingly, if you think there really is such a thing as genuine evil then you have a powerful argument for the reality of God.[2]

I'm not saying you can't be an atheist and a good person.

I'm just asking, "Without God, what does 'good' even mean?"

Christianity isn't about being a good person; it's about being a broken person who follows the best Person. The grace of Jesus redeems the Bad within us and, over time, restores us until we reflect the image of our loving God.

Today's Scripture

"He has shown you, O man, what is good; And what does the Lord require of you But to do justly, To love mercy, And to walk humbly with your God?" (Micah 6:8 NKJV)

"Let love be without hypocrisy. Abhor what is evil. Cling to what is good." (Romans 12:9 NKJV)

Today's Prayer

I give You my whole heart today.
I give You my thoughts, my wants, my ambitions,
Because only You can make them good again.

DAY 38

WHY DON'T CHURCHES *DO* MORE GOOD?

I t never fails. First, a tragedy occurs—a storm, an earthquake, a shooting—leaving multiple people injured or dead. Then come the social media posts from Christians:

> #PrayforSandyHook
> #PrayersforHouston
> #PrayingforLasVegas

And then nobody ever seems to *do* anything. Many Christians, in particular, seem content to merely offer up our "thoughts and prayers" in a tweet or a meme. But Jesus wasn't much for lip service; He cared more about taking action. *So why don't churches do more to help people?*

After a recent terrorist attack in Paris, a popular meme made the rounds on social media: "Stop praying for Paris," it read, "and start fighting religious extremism." One Reddit user wrote, "People pray because it's easy, quick, free, and it absolves personal responsibility. Getting off your knees and working for change is hard, time-consuming, costly, and assumes personal responsibility. Prayer changes nothing, but we can change everything."

So let's think about what these people are saying: (1) Prayer never works, (2) those who pray for change never work for it, and (3) people can fix the world without God.

But is there really proof that prayer never works, or is the person who makes that claim really taking a leap of faith? Is there any *evidence* that people who pray don't work for change, or are we just being cynical about religion? And if people can fix the world without God, then why do secular societies still have problems—and why, when religion has been outlawed by those in power (for example, Stalin's Soviet Union, Mao's China), have human suffering and state-sanctioned brutality so dramatically increased?

Prayer can mean calling on God to intervene in your time of need, but it can also mean asking Him to give *you* the courage to intervene. Jesus taught His disciples to pray for God's will to "be done, on earth as it is in heaven" (Matthew 6:10) and then He told them to do God's will (see Matthew 7:21; 12:50).

In their book *Fearfully and Wonderfully Made*, Dr. Paul Brand and Philip Yancey share the story of a group of German college students who, in the aftermath of World War II, volunteered to help rebuild a massive cathedral in England that had been reduced to rubble by German bombs:

> As the work progressed, debate broke out on how to best restore a large statue of Jesus with His arms outstretched and bearing the familiar inscription, "Come unto me." Careful patching could repair all damage to the statue except for Christ's hands, which had been destroyed by bomb fragments. Should they attempt the delicate task of reshaping those hands? Finally the workers reached a decision that still stands today. The statue of Jesus has no hands, and the inscription now reads, "Christ has no hands but ours."[3]

Prayer works, and the one who prays, works. For followers of Jesus, there's no distinction here: prayer is nothing without work, and work is empty without prayer. Life with Jesus is never passive, for we are His hands in the world. Even when you are praying alone in your room, you are waging an assault against forces of darkness, negativity, and complacency.

I could do without all the post-traumatic hashtags, but I don't want to conceive of a world where people stop praying about our problems. Faithful prayer is always the beginning of a revolution. It begins with you, broken and on your knees, begging God for help, and it ends with you standing strong, helping others who are broken and on their knees.

What are you waiting for? Pray, and get to work.

Today's Scripture

"Pray without ceasing." (1 Thessalonians 5:17 NKJV)

"The prayer of a righteous person is powerful and effective." (James 5:16)

Today's Prayer

Sometimes it feels like I'm surrounded by brokenness and need. Help me today to see the best ways to help those in need. Thank You.

DAY 39

WHY WOULD ANY PARENTS FORCE RELIGION ONTO THEIR KIDS?

In a featured story on CNN.com, Deborah Mitchell, a mother of two in Texas, shared all the reasons why she refuses to raise her kids to believe in God. Citing reasons like "God is not logical," "God is not fair," "God is not present," and "God teaches narcissism," Mitchell insisted that the only reason people believe in an "imaginary" God is because the idea that we're alone in the universe is too horrifying for some people to handle. Seemingly writing out of frustration and loneliness, as she offered no coherent arguments to support her claims, Mitchell insinuated that the only honest way to raise a child is without God.[4]

I think most people feel that having religion (or not) should be a choice everyone makes for themselves. According to this way of thinking, parents who push a specific religion onto their kids rob them of the freedom to choose their own path. Wouldn't a more responsible approach to parenting be to raise kids who are respectful of all belief systems? That way, as kids grow up, good parents can encourage them to make their own choices about what they believe to be true.

Why would anyone force their religion onto their kids?

In my daughter's third-grade class, there are six kids with MAGA hats, eighteen devastated Democrats, three perpetually hungry vegans, five perpetually frustrated Texas Longhorn football fans, at least two avowed atheists, several recycling evangelists, and maybe a dozen kids who *know* the Tooth Fairy isn't real, and they're on a holy crusade to convert other students to their disbelief in such a fanciful myth.

All parenting is indoctrination. Every parent raises kids to believe in *something*—even Deborah Mitchell. Parents raising kids to be "open-minded" and to "make their own choices about what they believe" brain-wash their kids no less than those who drag their children to church every Sunday. The question isn't *whether or how* we're proselytizing our children; the question is, What are we teaching them about Truth?

With or without religion, all parents instill in our kids a belief system built on foundational truth claims. Many people raising vegetarian kids are passing down their convictions about health, sustainability, and the humane treatment of animals—truth claims they hope their kids will live by. For some parents of teenagers, nothing is more important than academic achievement; earning the best grades, staying involved in top-notch extracurriculars, and getting into the "right school" becomes the ultimate goal. These parents communicate certain truths to their kids about what *really* matters in this life—and what doesn't.

Not all live-and-let-live parents are as militant as Mitchell; some simply prefer not to teach their kids anything about ultimate Truth. But in doing so, they still communicate specific truth claims to their children:

- religion only matters insofar as it makes you a good person,
- all religions are equally true and/or equally untrue,
- being a "good person" is the highest ideal.

These assumptions are easy to deconstruct:

- religions aren't self-help techniques; they're Truth claims;
- all religions make different Truth claims, so it's logically impossible for them to be equally true and/or untrue;
- what makes a person "good"? Can everyone define *good* on their own terms?

What if, according to my worldview, "good" means educating my sons but not my daughters? If it's *good* for *me*, does that mean it's ultimately good? Most people would say no. It's not right that boys would receive an education while girls don't. But what gives you the right to impose your version of truth onto someone else?

Our belief in the equality and basic rights of little girls is nonnegotiable. But why? Because some things in this world are ultimately true. Relativism—the belief that we should all live and let live—crumbles under the weight of real-life situations.

All parents raise their kids with some notion of Truth. Christian parents hope to raise Christian kids because we believe the Jesus-centered worldview is ultimately true. More than anything, we long for our kids to know God created them, cares for them, forgives them, heals them, redeems them, and calls them to love and serve their neighbors, especially the poor and broken among them.

I'm desperate for my kids to know the Truth of God's love and grace. Call it brainwashing if you want; maybe sometimes our brains need washing.

Today's Scripture

"Train up a child in the way he should go, And when he is old he will not depart from it." (Proverbs 22:6 NKJV)

"Then children were brought to him that he might lay his hands on them and pray. The disciples rebuked the people, but Jesus said, 'Let the little children come to me and do not hinder them, for to such belongs the kingdom of heaven.' And he laid his hands on them and went away." (Matthew 19:13-15 ESV)

Today's Prayer

I don't want to raise religious kids; I just want to live according to my convictions that Jesus is the Truth, that You are Love, that I am forgiven, and that this life matters.

DAY 40

WHAT DIFFERENCE DOES JESUS MAKE?

Even if you believe Jesus came back from the dead, you should be able to explain what difference it makes today. The typical Christian responses leave most agnostics and skeptics feeling cold. Some believers say, "Jesus rose to fulfill Old Testament prophecy," which sounds an awful lot like circular logic. The Bible says a thing happened... to prove that the Bible was true when it predicted that thing was going to happen. Even my seven-year-old knows that line of reasoning lacks credibility.

Others say, "Without the Resurrection there would be no salvation." OK—but salvation from what? Sin and death? I thought Jesus conquered sin and death by His sacrifice on the cross? Shouldn't the cross have been enough for my sins to be forgiven? Why was resurrection even necessary?

It seems like, if the one true God really walked among us, died on a cross, and rose from the dead, the world should have changed by now. Many Christians can't identify any significant ways the resurrection of Jesus has made anything substantially better. There was just as much poverty, disease, and war the day after the first Easter as there was the day before.

So yeah, Jesus was an extraordinary human being, and some people have good reasons to believe in His resurrection, but even if it's true, who cares? What difference did it make?

Jesus didn't rise from the dead just to prove the Bible was right. He also didn't come back from the dead so our sins will be forgiven; we believe that happened on the cross. But if that's where the story ends—with Jesus's dead body—who would care about having their sins forgiven? Forgiven for what? To what end? So we can all die with a clear conscience? If Jesus's dead, rotting body is still in the ground somewhere, He is the Bernie Madoff of world religions. On the other hand, if the Resurrection is actually true, it's the only thing that really matters.

The people who encountered Jesus after the Resurrection weren't just amazed by a miracle; they were intoxicated by something. And whatever that *something* was, they were all suddenly willing to die for it. What was it? Hope. Because God hadn't come near to them just to teach them or amaze them or even just to forgive them. Jesus overcame death so we can all overcome death, which is why the first Christians were so unafraid to die.

I could spend several pages on all the ways the resurrection of Jesus has improved quality of life in the "real world." For example, the roles and rights of women have progressed dramatically since Jesus rose and appeared first to women—trusting them to share the biggest news in history. For two millennia, Jesus's followers have served the poor, healed the sick, visited prisoners, and changed the world like no other group before or since. It was Jesus who inspired the anti-apartheid revolution in South Africa. During their push for equality, Nelson Mandela, Desmond Tutu, and other Christian leaders insisted on loving their enemies instead of merely punishing them. Of that time, Tutu wrote,

> Many people believe that they are beyond God's love—that God may love others but that what they have done has caused God to stop loving them. But Jesus by His example showed us that God loves sinners as much as saints. . . .
>
> I saw the power of this gospel when I was serving as chairperson of the Truth and Reconciliation Commission, . . . [which] gave

perpetrators of political crimes the opportunity to appeal for amnesty by telling the truth of their actions and ... to ask for forgivenesss. ...

As we listened to accounts of truly monstrous deeds of torture and cruelty, it would have been easy to dismiss the perpetrators as monsters. ... But we are reminded that God's love is not cut off from anyone. ...

We cannot condemn anyone to being irredeemable, as Jesus reminded us on the Cross, crucified as he was between two thieves. ... He does not give up on you or on anyone, for God loves you now and will always love you.[5]

But that's nothing compared to the difference Easter makes in the heart of a person who believes. Because when you have hope, you're not afraid to die. And when you're not afraid to die, you're free to love with reckless abandon.

Jesus marched out of His tomb to lead the rest of us out of ours. Life beyond death is the reason he rose. Because Jesus rose, we all can rise.

Today's Scripture

"Do not let your hearts be troubled. You believe in God; believe also in me. My Father's house has many rooms; if that were not so, would I have told you that I am going there to prepare a place for you? And if I go and prepare a place for you, I will come back and take you to be with me that you also may be where I am." (Jesus, in John 14:1-3)

"For if, while we were God's enemies, we were reconciled to him through the death of his Son, how much more, having been reconciled, shall we be saved through his life!" (Romans 5:10)

Today's Prayer

Thank You for dying on the cross. Thank You for rising from the grave. And thank You for showing the rest of us the way out of our own tombs. Help me to live with fearless hope today. Thank You.

BONUS: DAY 41

WHY CAN'T I BE A PRIVATE CHRISTIAN?

Some days, all my doubts meet their match, and I believe—in God, Jesus, the gospel, all of it—like when I experience something so beautiful that I'm moved to tears and thoughts of transcendence. Or when I think about existence—the universe, Earth, us—I *know* it didn't happen accidentally, without cause. I know it couldn't have. Or when I reflect on the mystery of love—a force that can never be proven in a lab but is so obviously, universally *true.*

The other day I heard two young women talking at a coffee shop. One of them has a newborn niece who might never make it home from the hospital. And during the conversation, the other woman said, "I'll be sending positive thoughts your way" at least five times.

What's a "positive thought" and where do you send it? And what good does a positive thought do? It was so obvious that she wanted to say, "I'll pray for your niece," but she couldn't bring herself to say it, so she said "I'll send positive thoughts" instead. Like me, she *knew* there is something more than just this material world. She *knew* there's something unseen that makes sending "positive thoughts" worthwhile. But she didn't want to be branded "religious."

Sometimes skeptics become believers, but they'd rather not admit it. They're too proud to tell their Christian family and friends because they can't stomach all the self-righteous "I told you sos." And they'd never tell their intellectual atheist friends and family because they're afraid of never getting invited to parties anymore.

So why can't the person believe without becoming a believer? Why can't someone privately love Jesus without publicly becoming a Christian?

Pride may be the leading cause of atheism and agnosticism today. The more you learn about the origins of the universe, the more you research the life, death, and resurrection of Jesus, the more you experience love, grace, and awe, the more likely you are to believe in a Creator and in the absolute Truth of the gospel.

But you can't start calling yourself a Christian, because you've spent years calling Christians irrational, anti-science hillbillies (or some variation of that). That's your pride getting in the way.

Look, becoming a Christian doesn't mean changing political parties, boycotting Bill Nye, rooting for Tim Tebow, and swapping out all your fun friends for a bunch of goody-two-shoe Bible thumpers. All it means is "community."

A brilliant man named John Wesley said, "There is no such thing as a solitary Christian." The phrase itself is a contradiction in terms, as Christianity is necessarily a communal act.

I know Christians can be a little much sometimes. There are certain *kinds* of Christians I'd rather not spend much time around (I'm hoping there are separate rooms in heaven). But there are also some really amazing churches out there, full of sincere, down-to-earth people; you just have to look for them.

I recently had the privilege of baptizing several people on a Sunday morning, and part of the ceremony involved the whole congregation promising to love, support, and care for each person being baptized. If you've never sat in a room full of people as they swear an oath to unconditionally love and nurture a baby and her parents for their *entire lives*—and they mean it—you're missing out.

Or if you've never sat in a living room with a small group of people who gather to eat, drink, and follow Jesus together—keeping one another in sacred covenant and holding one another accountable in love—it's a beautiful thing to behold.

Or if you've never gone to serve a meal to homeless people or spent time in prisons with other Christians visiting inmates, you've yet to witness the gospel at its best.

Swallow your pride, search for a church that fits you, and dive in. Stop sending positive thoughts and start praying. Don't worry about what other people will think or say, and simply act on what you *know*: God is real, the gospel is true, and your life has purpose beyond what you can see.

Today's Scripture

"Then you will know the truth, and the truth will set you free."

(Jesus, in John 8:32)

"Therefore, if anyone is in Christ, he is a new creation; old things have passed away; behold, all things have become new." (2 Corinthians 5:17)

Today's Prayer

I'm a believer. It's true. So help me follow Your ways today. Lead me toward a community of other believers where I can grow in faith. And when I find that community, give me the courage to shun cynicism and dive right in. Thank You!

Notes

1. Doubts About God

1. Sam Harris, *Letter to a Christian Nation* (New York: Knopf, 2006), 73.

2. Harris, *Letter to a Christian Nation*, 23.

3. G. K. Chesterton, *Orthodoxy* (West Valley City, UT: Waking Lion, 2008), 24.

4. Chesterton, *Orthodoxy*, 24.

5. David Foster Wallace, *This Is Water*, Commencement address delivered May 21, 2005, at Kenyon College, Gambier, Ohio.

6. Stephen Hawking, interview by Larry King, *Larry King Live*, September 10, 2010, www.cnn.com/videos/us/2018/03/14/stephen-hawking-2010 -larry-king-live-intv-sot.cnn/video/playlists/intl-from-the-us/.

7. N. T. Wright, "Getting Started: Stating the Modern Case" in *Belief: Readings on the Reason for Faith*, ed. Francis S. Collins (New York: HarperOne, 2010), 3.

8. Eric Huffman, interview with Bart Campolo, "Why Do People Love to Hate Religion?" podcast audio, *Maybe God with Eric Huffman*, January 10, 2018.

9. Joy Behar, *The View*, aired February 13, 2018, on ABC.

2. Doubts About Jesus

1. Dr. Michael C. LaBossiere, "42 Fallacies: Ad Hominem" (PDF), 2, Trivium Education, www. triviumeducation.com/texts/42Fallacies.pdf.

2. Bart D. Ehrman, *Did Jesus Exist? The Historical Argument for Jesus of Nazareth* (San Francisco: HarperOne, 2012), 96.

3. Marcus Borg, *The Resurrection of Jesus: "Physical/Bodily" or "Spiritual/Mystical,"* The Marcus J. Borg Foundation, May 16, 2011, https://marcusjborg.org/the-resurrection-of-jesus/.

3. Doubts About the Bible

1. Madeleine L'Engle, *The Rock That Is Higher* (Colorado Springs: WaterBrook, 2002), 88.

2. Martin Luther King Jr., "A Tough Mind and a Tender Heart," sermon delivered in Atlanta, GA, in August 1959, www.thekingcenter.org/archive/document/tough-mind-and-tender-heart-1#.

4. Doubts About the Human Condition

1. Phillip Yancey, *What's So Amazing about Grace?* (New York: HarperCollins, 1997), 299.

2. Blaise Pascal, *Pensées* (New York: E. P. Dutton, 1958).

3. C. S. Lewis, quoted in Timothy Keller, *The Reason for God: Belief in an Age of Skepticism* (London: Penguin, 2008), 81.

4. Yann Martel, *The Life of Pi* (Boston: Mariner, 2003), 35.

5. Doubts About Faith and Science

1. Thomas Jefferson, "To William Short, Monticello, August 4, 1820," personal letter, American History website, www.let.rug.nl/usa/presidents/thomas-jefferson/letters-of-thomas-jefferson/jefl261.php.

2. Thomas Jefferson, *The Jefferson Bible: The Life and Morals of Jesus of Nazareth* (Boston: Beacon, 1989).

3. Thomas Jefferson, "Thomas Jefferson to John Trumbull," personal

letter, February 15, 1789, Library of Congress website, www.loc.gov/exhib
its/jefferson/18.html.

4. Carl Sagan, *Cosmos* (New York: Random House, 1980), 4.

5. Anthony Flew, *There Is a God: How the World's Most Notorious Atheist
Changed His Mind* (San Francisco: HarperOne, 2008), 88.

6. Dr. Lawrence Krauss, in a public debate with Dr. William Lane Craig,
The City Bible Forum, Brisbane, Australia, August 2013, www.youtube
.com/watch?v=Qb1-F_UEtS4 (01:33:00—1:37-46).

7. Richard Dawkins, interview by Ben Stein, *Expelled: No Intelligence
Allowed*, directed by Nathan Frankowski (Vivendi Entertainment, Rocky
Mountain Pictures, 2008).

8. Lawrence Krauss, "A Universe without Purpose," *Los Angeles Times*,
April 1, 2012.

9. John Polkinghorne, *Belief in God in an Age of Science* (New Haven: Yale
University Press, 2003), 1.

10. Richard Dawkins, *The Ancestor's Tale: A Pilgrimage to the Dawn of Life*
(Boston: Houghton Mifflin, 2004), 756.

11. Francis Collins, *Belief: Readings on the Reason for Faith* (San Francisco:
HarperOne, 2010), xv.

12. G. K. Chesterton, *Orthodoxy* (West Valley City, UT: Waking Lion
Press, 2008), 26.

13. Scott J. Jones and Arthur Jones, *Ask: Faith Questions in a Skeptical Age*
(Nashville: Abingdon Press, 2015), 52.

14. Stephen Jay Gould, "Impeaching a Self-Appointed Judge," *Scientific
American* 267, no. 1 (July 1992): 118–21.

15. William Ryan and Walter Pitman, *Noah's Flood: The New Scientific
Discoveries About the Event That Changed History* (New York: Simon &
Schuster; Touchstone edition, 2000).

6. Doubts About Quality of Life

1. The Acts of Paul 2:3, written by an anonymous presbyter of Asia, ca. AD 160. Quoted in Stephen Miller, "Bald, Blind & Single?" *Christian History* 47: *The Apostle Paul and His Times* (1995), *Christianity Today*, www.christianitytoday.com/history/issues/issue-47/on-road-with-paul.html.

2. Viktor Frankl, *Man's Search for Meaning* (Boston: Beacon, 2006), 115.

3. John Wesley, *A Covenant Prayer*, 1755.

4. David Kinnaman, *unChristian: What a New Generation Really Thinks about Christianity... and Why It Matters* (Grand Rapids: Baker Books, 2012), 34.

7. Doubts About Sex and Relationships

1. St. Jerome, *Against Jovinianus*, as quoted in *Nicene and Post-Nicene Fathers of the Christian Church*, Second Series, vol. 6, ed. Philip Schaff, trans. W. H. Fremantle (Grand Rapids: Eerdmans, 1979), 922.

2. Debra Hirsch, *Redeeming Sex: Naked Conversations about Sexuality and Spirituality* (Downers Grove, IL: IVP Books, 2015), 120.

3. Eric Huffman, interview with Debra Hirsch, "Can Sex Bring Us Closer to God?" podcast audio, *Maybe God with Eric Huffman*, January 25, 2018.

4. David Kinnaman, *unChristian: What a New Generation Really Thinks about Christianity... and Why It Matters* (Grand Rapids: Baker, 2012), 34.

5. C. S. Lewis, *Mere Christianity*, rev. and enlarged ed. (San Francisco: HarperOne, 2015), 84.

8. Doubts About Religion

1. Ricky Gervais (@rickygervais), "I've never been insulted," Twitter, May 19, 2013, 1:27 p.m., https://twitter.com/rickygervais/status/336216574174302208?lang=en.

2. Alvin Plantinga, "A Christian Life Partly Lived," *Philosophers Who Believe*, ed. Kelly James Clark (Downers Grove, IL: Intervarsity Press, 1993), 73.

3. Philip Yancey and Paul Brand, *Fearfully and Wonderfully Made* (Grand Rapids: Zondervan, 1997), 206.

4. Deborah Mitchell, *Why I Raise My Children without God*, CNN.com, January 15, 2013, http://religion.blogs.cnn.com/2013/01/15/ireport-why -i-raise-my-children-without-god/.

5. Desmond Tutu, *God Has a Dream: A Vision of Hope for Our Time* (New York: Image Books, 2005), 10–11.